MODERN TIMES

Modern Africa
1870–1970

Titles in this series

MODERN TIMES

Modern Africa
1870 – 1970

Barry Williams

GILLINGHAM SCHOOL, DORSET

LONGMAN

LONGMAN GROUP LIMITED
London

*Associated companies, branches and representatives
throughout the world*

© Longman Group Ltd 1970

First published 1970
Third impression 1972

ISBN 0 582 20429 1

*Printed in Hong Kong by
Sheck Wah Tong Printing Press Ltd*

For David Rubadiri

Acknowledgements

We are indebted to the following for permission to reproduce copyright material:
Routledge & Kegan Paul Limited for an extract from *African Women* by Sylvia Leith-
Ross.

The author and publisher are grateful to the following for permission to reproduce
photographs:

Associated Press Ltd., page 79; Anti-Slavery Society for Protection of Human Rights,
page 11, *left and right*; B.B.C. Publications, page 112, based on a map in their publica-
tion, *Africa*, 1968, page 28; Camera Press, pages 107, *centre and right*, and 122; Central
Office of Information: Crown copyright, page 139; Central Press, pages 80, 89 and
124; East Africa Railways and Harbours Board, page 82; F.A.O. Photo Unit, Rome,
pages 119 and 130; Rune Hassner, Stockholm, cover; John Hillelson Agency, page 70
and Ian Berry, Magnum, pages 147, 148, 150 and 151; Illustrated London News,
page 48; Kenya Information Services, page 90; H. Lhote: *The Search for the Tassili
Frescoes*, Hutchinson, 1959, page 2; Mansell Collection, page 125; National Archives
of Rhodesia, pages 6 and 31; Nigeria House Information Service, page 110; Paul
Popper, pages 32 *left*, 77, 84, 87 and 106, *left, centre and right*; Penguin Books Limited,
pages 4 and 50, adapted from maps in *Short History of Africa* by Oliver and Fage;
Pretoria State Information Service, page 33 *centre*; Punch Magazine, pages 20, 38, 58,
64, 96 and 159; Radio Times Hulton Picture Library, pages 16, 25, 32 *centre*, 33 *right*,
45 and 100; E. Sik: *History of Black Africa*: Volume I, Budapest, 1966: page 32 *right*;
Syndication International, photos by James Barr, pages 117 and 132; Twentieth
Century Fund, page 137; E. Waterlot: *Les Bas-Reliefs des Bâtiments Royaux d'Abomey*,
University of Paris, 1926, page 42.

Preface

Few of us realize how big and empty of people Africa is. It is quite easy to fit the outlines of West and Central Europe, the United States, India and China into the continent. Items of news from Africa in recent years have been concerned with two main issues: the relations between peoples of different skin colour; and the difficulties which newly independent nations face in establishing stable governments. These are thorny questions, and they sometimes obscure a very important third issue, the economic one of how Africa is to earn a prosperous living in the modern world.

This book, written for a younger generation of readers of the 15–19 age group, tries to sketch in the background to these issues over the last hundred years, and to describe a little of the situation as it is today. I hope some chapters are detailed enough for the reader to enjoy a depth of interest, but also that the book is short enough for the overall picture to be seen. It is a century of unique excitement, with so many changes compressed into such a short time. Unfortunately most British school texts present modern African history only as an appendage to European activities.

There are many difficulties in writing about Africa in the last century, and the author is fully aware of the shortcomings they may produce in a short book. The subject is so vast that a great deal of selection of material has been necessary, with the accompanying pitfall of the invalid generalization. Again, in recent times, the pace of events has been so swift that I am reminded of Elspeth Huxley's dilemma. When writing about East Africa she said she felt like an artist trying to draw a galloping horse; by the time the outline had been pencilled in, the subject was over the horizon.

Perhaps the most difficult problem is bias. Both European and African, white and black, viewpoints are given space, and I have tried to guard against the book becoming a document in which 'colonial rule' is put in the dock and evidence produced for its prosecution and defence. Also, today, *any* criticism of a poor, young, independent African nation might seem to support those who think independence was always granted too soon.

I should like to acknowledge a deep debt to the researches of the hundred or so authorities on Africa consulted in the writing of this book: from the social surveys and polemical tracts to the journalists' reports and sober historical assessments of writers like Guy Hunter, J. B. Marais, F. S. Oliver, J. D. Fage, Anthony Atmore, Rene Dumont, Ruth Slade, Colin Legum, Tom Little, John Hatch, Kofi Busia and to the many historians who have written for African publications like *Zamani* and *Tarikh*.

B.W.

Kington Magna, Dorset, September 1969

Contents

1 The Myth of Darkest Africa

European Ignorance

'O, how great is that darkness', wrote an English traveller about Africa in the middle of the nineteenth century. He was putting into words how most Europeans felt about Africa, just before the continent was extensively explored and partitioned by them. As late as 1898 a small book of verse called *The Modern Traveller* was selling well in London. The Victorians read

> Oh Africa, mysterious land!
> Surrounded by a lot of sand . . .

and learned that it was inhabited by 'savages called Tuaregs' and 'nasty, dirty Hottentots', and that it was full of elephants, lions and 'serpants, seven yards long at least'.

Yet, as one writer recently put it, 'the darkest thing about Africa has always been our ignorance of it'. In the eighteenth century Africa was only a coastline to Europeans. On maps the shape was roughly correct, but as Jonathan Swift wrote,

> So geographers, in Afric maps,
> With savage pictures fill the gaps;
> And o'er unhabitable downs
> Place elephants for want of towns.

Africa then was a place of fable and strange customs, and only occasionally did factual reports come to Europe from missionaries or merchants. Many of these men too gave the impression that they were heroes doing battle with cannibals and painted savages—the forces of darkness. A visitor to East Africa told of 'bloodstained misery, hopeless poverty and brutish, pagan life'. Was Old Africa really as backward and primitive as these contemporary European views would have us believe?

The Vigour of Old Africa

In agriculture, perhaps, there was only a little development. For centuries African peoples, in face of considerable difficulties like disease, extremes of climate and poor soil, have farmed the land only for their immediate needs. But in craft some of her peoples produced works of high artistry. Such African products were in demand abroad, and towns and ports grew up from a prosperous trade. Hindu brides of medieval India wore carved ivory from Kenya. Iron smelted in simple blast furnaces in East Africa gained an international reputation; a medieval document records that 'this East African iron went to all the lands of India at a good price because it is most superior in quality'. Recently, archaeologists have found evidence of at

A rock painting from the eastern Sahara region which dates from c 3,500 BC. Note the style of line drawing which could well have been done in the twentieth century!

least seven thousand old mine workings for iron and gold between the Zambesi and Limpopo rivers.

In the ten centuries before 1870 there were two great trading areas in Africa. The trans-Saharan routes ran from the Mediterranean coast to the Sudan kingdoms lying along the northern edge of the rain forests; and Indian Ocean routes took merchants from the East African coastline to India and China. Contemporary descriptions of two big trading cities show how prosperous some of this commerce was.

Kilwa, just south of Zanzibar, had three centuries of fame and wealth before the Portuguese destroyed it in 1505. A fourteenth-century Muslim scholar, Ibn Battuta, passed through it on his way from Morocco to China, and remarked; 'Kilwa is one of the most beautiful and well-constructed towns.' In 1964 a British archaeologist confirmed Battuta's statement. He found a fine group of buildings, with courtyards, good washing arrangements and a big eight-sided bathing pool.

Across the other side of Africa was Kano, in the northern part of modern Nigeria. In the early nineteenth century it was the main commercial and craft centre of the Hausa people. Its 30,000 population doubled annually during the January–April period when the Saharan caravans came in. Kano's markets were 'crowded from sunrise to sunset everyday', wrote travellers. The German explorer, Heinrich Barth, noted in 1851 that 'commerce and manufactures go hand in hand, and almost every family has its share in them.' Its manufactures were cloth, woven from locally-grown cotton and dyed blue, sandals and tanned hides. Kano cloth was famous as far as Morocco, Tripoli and Lagos. Clothing, carpets, silk, spices, books, horses, salt and copper were other products for which Kano acted as an entrepot.

Only a handful of Europeans like Barth showed an interest in African merchandise. Even greater ignorance existed about African politics. All peoples were thought of as 'tribes' with 'chiefs', yet the continent had many different forms of government. The large empires of Ghana, Mali and Songhai stretched across the savannah regions of West Africa in medieval times. The king of Ghana, with enough riches to put golden collars round his dogs' necks, was much wealthier than his contemporary in Anglo-Saxon England. Mali was a bigger state than any

3

Old Africa. The main tribal concentrations and some of the big empires which Africans built at different times in the thousand years before European colonization

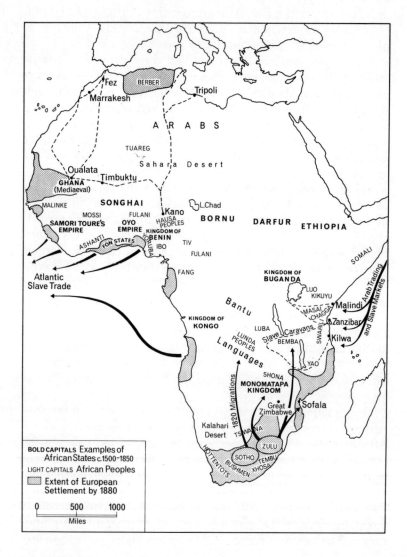

in medieval Europe, and had a well-organized money and taxation system. Later, the Portuguese described the sixteenth-century kingdom of the Kongo as 'great and powerful, full of people having many vassals'.

In central Africa in the mid-nineteenth century lay the Ba-Kuba kingdom. This had an advanced form of government. The king ruled with a group of ministers which included a prime minister, a minister of war, a representative from each of the four provinces of Ba-Kuba and two women, daughters of former kings. They were helped by a wide range of court officials, trade and gild delegates and twelve judges.

Africa has had a long history, full of change and movement. Old Africa was far from being the fearful place imagined by some nineteenth-century European writers. Why were they so unwilling to find out the truth?

Slaves and Machines

Early relations between Europeans and Africans—round about the fifteenth century—were those of equals. There were exceptions, as when the jealous Portuguese traders sacked East African ports like Kilwa, but the kingdoms of Benin (in modern Nigeria) and the Congo were greatly respected. A black ambassador 'of good speech and natural wisdom' represented Benin in Lisbon.

Later, Europeans adopted a superior attitude to Africa. There were many reasons for this, but two are especially important. The slave trade and its abolition was one. Different kinds of slavery had existed in Africa for centuries. In the Muslim states of North Africa it was regulated by law, so that a slave had both rights and status. Along the East African coast the Arabs controlled another kind—a wealthy overseas trade. By the nineteenth century slave 'caravans' went inland, bought slaves from local chiefs at about three shillings each, returned to a big coastal market and sold them for £6. The great Zanzibar slave market exported 20,000 a year to India and the East.

With the growth of the Atlantic Ocean trade Europeans entered the slave business. Slaves bound for American sugar, tobacco and cotton plantations were treated like animals. As time went on the skin colour of a person became significant, and

5

Mid-nineteenth century slave caravan from central Africa to an East African port

the equation made up by Europeans was thought to be quite normal: Black = Slave = Inferior; White = Free = Superior. The first slave ship crossed the Atlantic in 1519, the last entered Havana harbour in Cuba in 1865. Between these dates some six million Africans were shipped across the Atlantic. Phrases from slave ship journals like 'chains rattling', 'misery and distress' and 'the stench from the hold was scarcely bearable' give an idea of the appalling conditions.

White slave traders were willing to respect the independence of many African peoples, for they found they had no need to go into the African interior. It was more profitable to use local tribal rivalries. A warlike coastal people could easily be tempted to go inland and seize other Africans for barter. A log book of an eighteenth-century slave ship read: 'For a man and a girl— one roll of tobacco, one string of pipe coral, one gun, three cutlasses, one brass blunderbuss, twenty-four linen handkerchiefs, five patches of cloth, three jugs of rum, twelve pint mugs, one laced hat.' With the abolition of the slave trade by the European powers in the early nineteenth century, traders in produce like palm oil succeeded the slavers. These men wanted a more direct control of African peoples, and brings us to the next point.

The second reason hindering the proper development of Afro-European relations was the Industrial Revolution. The factories of Europe began to manufacture goods in great quantities and sometimes of better quality than Africans could produce. East African craft production decreased as the markets of Asia turned to Europe not Africa for some of its goods. Also the trans-Saharan caravan trade declined in the later nineteenth century after European traders and gunboats began moving up the rivers of West Africa to the interior. As one writer put it, 'The camel was no match for the steam vessel.'

With the adventurers and traders came the missionaries. All of them came from a Europe proud of its machinery and technical knowledge and confident of its power. Africa seemed very backward and inferior. More and more Europeans went to the continent feeling they were born to rule and that trade and religion must also be under their control. Some said they had a divine mission for this. The explorer, Livingstone, returned to early Victorian England with the firm idea that it was Europe's duty to take the three Cs to Africa, 'Christianity, Commerce and Civilization'. Others were quite willing to use force to bring about such a praiseworthy achievement. Later a music-hall version of the famous Christian hymn became popular in West Africa.

> Onward Christian soldiers, unto heathen lands,
> Prayer books in your pockets, rifles in your hand;
> Take the happy tidings where trading can be done,
> Spread the peaceful gospel with the Gatling gun.

Until the late 1870s the movement of Europeans into Africa was limited to these explorers, missionaries and merchants. Governments showed little interest. But in the last quarter of the nineteenth century possession of an empire became a badge of a nation's superiority. The situation changed dramatically. Europeans rushed to stake claim to huge areas. The speed with which they did this and partitioned the continent between them led it to be called 'the scramble for Africa'.

Yet Africans themselves had few illusions about the scramble. With thoughts of the slave trade, the Lagos editor of an African newspaper wrote in 1891: 'A forcible possession of our land has taken the place of the forcible possession of our persons.'

2

2 Selfish Colonialism in the Congo

Leopold, King of the Belgians

King Leopold was an energetic and ambitious man. He was also, said the explorer, Stanley, 'a dreamer of dreams'. In the small state of Belgium he felt he was a king with too little to do, and when he failed to get his government to support him in his ideas he decided to go ahead on his own.

He fixed his attention on Africa where he had thoughts of empire-building. He planned many things, but two of them attracted his special efforts: the extermination of the Arab slave trade and the control of the rubber and ivory trade of the Congo region. The first of these he hoped would give him a reputation as a 'nineteenth-century crusader'. There is no doubt that Leopold, as a young man, was an idealist, genuinely concerned with ending the widespread Arab slaving in East and Central Africa. He wanted to do so much, but he had little money of his own. Also, as he grew older, he developed a personal taste for wealth and power. The Congo seemed the place to get both, for no European power had shown much interest in the area.

So, in 1876, Leopold founded the International Association for Exploration and Civilization in Africa. It is often difficult to date the beginning of a complicated series of events, but in the 'scramble for Africa' this year was to prove a really significant one.

Leopold was fortunate. Another man showed him the trading possibilities of the Congo: Henry Morton Stanley. Born in Wales he had worked his passage as a boy across the Atlantic to America and become a journalist-explorer. He made his name when the *New York Herald* newspaper asked him to find Livingstone, whose source of the Nile expedition had not been heard of for three years. After this success in 1871, he added to his prestige as an explorer by charting the long and difficult course of the Congo river. At this point, in 1879, he entered the service of King Leopold, who was willing to put up the money for one of Stanley's trading schemes.

The Berlin Conference on Africa, 1884

The lower part of the great River Congo (i.e. below Stanley Pool) has many waterfalls and cataracts which make it impossible for navigation. But the middle reach of the river (i.e. up to Stanley Falls), with its many tributaries, gives excellent navigation over a total of 4,000 miles in Central Africa. In fact it was easier to trade and travel eastwards to the Indian Ocean than to move over the shorter distance to the Atlantic.

Leopold and Stanley decided to build a road and railway from near the mouth of the Congo up to Stanley Pool, and here launch steamboats to attract the rich trade of the Congo Basin. It seemed a great vision to them, to swing the trade of Central Africa away from Arab control in the east to the Atlantic and Europe. This trade would, of course, be under Leopold's supervision.

However, by the mid-1880s other European nations were showing interest in the commercial possibilities of central and also West Africa. A conference of statesmen met to discuss these matters in 1884 in Berlin. Here Leopold argued that his 'international' Congo Association would guarantee freedom of trade in the region. This seemed a satisfactory solution, for the European governments by now were too busy and suspicious of each other elsewhere in Africa to worry about Leopold's ultimate intentions. British and French rivalry in West Africa was particularly acute.

The Europeans at Berlin in 1884 knew little about the people who lived in the Congo. No one had thought Stanley's remark at the Conference in any way unusual. He said, 'The Association has 450 treaties with African chiefs, who of their own free will have transferred their rights of ownership to the Association.' Nobody questioned whether the Africans needed anyone to look after their interests in such 'bargains', because many Europeans took the view of a Congo missionary who declared: 'the African race is cursed of God. Those black pagans are lazy, greedy, thieves and liars.'

People of the Congo

How far was this a fair verdict on the people of the Congo region? There were two main groups, pygmies and Bantu-speaking Negroes. The first and the smaller lived like nomads in the forest regions. Theirs was a hand-to-mouth existence, the women gathering fruit, nuts and roots, and the men hunting animals. They kept very much to themselves, avoiding both white man and Bantu African.

Although many Negro tribes of the Congo spoke similar languages called Bantu, there were often great differences in looks. Not all had woolly hair, and the colour of the skin varied from coal-black, through chocolate-brown to ash-grey. The Congo Bantu lived in settled villages and grew their own food in forest clearings. They also had a tradition of high skill in arts and crafts. A German explorer, Leo Frobenius, wrote:

'In the Congo I penetrated the region of the Kasai and found villages where the principal streets were lined on both sides, miles on end, with four rows of palm trees. There was not a man who did not carry sumptuous weapons of iron and copper. Everywhere were velvets and silken clothes, and pieces of artistry worthy of comparison with the creations of Europe.'

This was not unusual, but the Congo region had thousands of small villages, many of which were almost completely cut off from the outside world. And there were many untrustworthy rogues about. It is clear that too many Europeans were prepared to believe the few horror tales which missionaries and explorers brought back, and to think all Africa was like that.

Exploitation

The verb 'to exploit' has two slightly different meanings: it can mean 'to work on something and use it properly'; it is also used to describe the 'seizing and using of land and people for selfish purposes'. That Leopold intended the second soon became clear to the people of the Congo.

In 1885 Leopold issued a declaration saying 'all vacant land belongs to the Congo State' (that is, himself). In theory the people should pay taxes so that the ivory and rubber wealth of the 'vacant' Congo forests could be worked. But as there was no common tribal currency the tax took the form of 'labour': the Congolese peoples had to go out and collect the rubber and ivory without payment. Leopold sent out agents from Belgium to supervise this work, for which there were no set hours. Also the agents were encouraged to get as much work as they could

A Congo atrocity: a foot has been cut off as a penalty for not bringing in enough rubber

THE KING OF THE RUBBERNECKS.

MORE RUBBER.

KING LEOPOLD of BELGIUM

CONGO FREE STATE

John Bull watch the King of the Rubbernecks with non-committal expressions

out of the Congolese. In 1891 Leopold issued another declaration saying it was 'the first duty of officials to raise revenue for the State'. In return the agents were promised that the more rubber and ivory they collected the more they would be paid. To many of the agents this was an obvious invitation to use force! A contemporary commented, 'Has anyone ever heard of a more direct incentive to robbery and violence?'

The system worked as follows. One of Leopold's agents would arrive by canoe at a group of villages with some hired African soldiers. They set up a few huts called an 'out-station', and raided the nearby villages. Native huts were looted for food, and wives and young children seized and taken to a 'hostage-house', one of the huts at the out-station. They were only returned when a man had collected a required load of rubber. Life in the hostage-house was appalling. A traveller told of women 'chained and herded like cattle into a pen and half-starved'; a missionary said, 'I staggered back as I entered, from the odour which belched forth. The faces turned upwards —hollow cheeks, misery and terror in their eyes.'

The rest of the family, such as cousins and old aunts and uncles had to bake 'kwango', a kind of bread, which then had to be taken every four days in great loads to the soldiers of the out-station or to European settlements, perhaps twenty miles distant.

The rubber collection expected of a family was about twenty big basket loads twice a month. As one man might take about ten days to collect these twenty loads, a husband had to take his eldest boys and any unmarried brothers with him. They had to go deep into the forest to find the wild rubber vines—perhaps a two day journey. Here they built a rough shelter as protection against leopards, and collected rubber for three days before returning to the out-station. Only then would a family be re-united in the village, and be able to work together on its own fields. As this process occurred twice a month family life quickly broke up.

If a man was late, or the quantity of his rubber collection small, or its quality poor a vicious penalty was imposed. Some kind of mutilation took place. Usually one of his hands, or that of one of his family, was cut off. In the case of one notorious agent the man was shot on the spot. An English explorer moving along the eastern Congo region found 'whole districts administered by incompetent officials and troops of the lowest type of native, almost invariably cannibals. Villages were burnt to the ground and there were skeletons everywhere.' By the mid-1890s Leopold's agents had brought a reign of terror to the Congo.

Judgment

Slowly by the turn of the century evidence of what was going on in the Congo became more widely known. In Belgium people protested, but Leopold ignored them. In Britain a vigorous campaign was launched by Edmund Morel in 1900. Morel had collected a large number of accounts from traders, missionaries and explorers, and he called the whole episode 'one enormous fraud'. He worked out that in' fifteen years Leopold had made a profit of £5 million—none of which had been used for the benefit of the Congo. The British government then sent Roger Casement on an official eleven-week fact-finding mission. As he travelled Casement wrote: 'The daily agony of an entire people unrolled itself in all the repulsive, terrifying details.' This humanitarian agitation against Leopold was very useful to European and American merchants, who saw that an attack on Leopold would allow them to put a finger in the rich Congo commercial pie, and possibly pull out a plum!

Leopold protested that he did not know about the misery and starvation. In any case he claimed that the Berlin Conference had granted him sovereignty—that is the right to rule. He took this to mean complete personal control in the Congo, and rudely answered his critics: 'No one possesses any right of intervention.'

Yet Leopold was an absentee landlord; he never once visited his vast property. He relied on agents, most of whom were unconcerned with the human suffering. A few were genuinely shocked at the conditions, but found they could not resign and that they would be sent to prison for desertion if they tried to leave the Congo.

Feelings against Leopold rose steadily in Western European countries, and in America, until in 1908 he agreed to give up his possession. Reluctantly, on 15 November, the Belgian government took over the administration of the Congo. Leading politicians in Brussels said they were unhappy at their 'blood-stained gift'. Leopold died in the following year. In the past twenty-four years he could claim to have opened up the Congo to explorers and merchants, and to have ended the Arab slave trade. But the methods of his agents led a recent writer to deliver the judgment: 'He was by all standards, personal and political, a rotten king.'

3 Britain in Egyptian Quicksand

The Suez Canal

In 1869 the Suez Canal was opened. It had been designed by Ferdinand de Lesseps, and had taken ten years to construct. Although planned for Egypt's benefit, de Lesseps' French company was given a 99-year lease on the land around the Canal and allowed to use forced labour for building. At one time 20,000 Egyptians were working under the whip; thousands died from exposure and bad food.

The ruler of Egypt at this time was the Khedive Ismail. The Canal was a key part of his great dream: a modernized, wealthy and internationally respected Egypt. Whilst the Canal construction was progressing, he bought a fleet of steamships for use on the Red Sea; he employed an English explorer, Baker, who had been searching for routes linking Egypt with the big African kingdoms and tribal areas of the upper Nile and Lake Victoria area; he planned irrigation schemes and a railway network. To pay for all this Ismail invited wealthy European investors and bankers to help him. Immense sums of money were loaned—but only at high rates of interest, because Ismail's reputation as an administrator was suspect. He was known to like a life of luxury.

The Canal was opened, but Europeans soon found that Ismail could manage neither his own money, nor the State's, efficiently. He ran into debt. He tried to cover up by more borrowing, but in 1876 his main supporters in Paris, Berlin and London refused to lend him any more. He already owed £90 million. His most valuable asset was his shares in the Suez Canal: seven-sixteenths of the total. He offered to sell these and the British government under Disraeli quickly seized the chance.

For the canal was proving of prime importance to Britain and it would be useful to have some control of it. It has been called 'the richest ditch on earth', and Britain valued it highly as a quick route for her trade to the Far East and as a passageway to India. To the Victorians India was the great base of their power

Port Said 1869: a combined fleet of the nations at the opening ceremony of the Suez Canal

and influence in the East. British merchants had hundreds of millions of pounds invested there. Also there was the Indian Army of a quarter of a million men, which made India, as one contemporary M.P. put it, 'an English barracks in the Oriental Seas'. Just over ten years after the Canal had been opened 82 per cent of the trade passing through was British.

Ismail's sale of the shares paid only some of his debts. By 1879 the Egyptian treasury was bankrupt. To protect all the money invested in the Canal and Egypt the French and the British, although rivals in trade, demanded that Ismail must go. His son, Tewfik, succeeded him, but the foreigners set up a dual control system of finance. British and French government officials would supervise Egyptian spending. Some of the big European bankers thought Britain and France should actually occupy Egypt, but the British refused to consider the idea. Apart from the Canal, they said, the rest of the country would be 'a useless encumbrance'.

The Revolt of Arabi Pasha

Under dual control Tewfik was merely a Franco-British puppet. The power of the Khedive in Egypt had always depended on the support of government officials, wealthy landowners and army generals. The most important of these people were of

Turkish descent and were very unpopular with the Egyptians. So, when the British insisted on money reforms, Tewfik became a 'debt-collector' for the foreigner. The land-tax was increased and many army officers were put on half-pay.

The effect was immediate. An Egyptian army colonel, Arabi Pasha, took a stand against the foreigners—the Turk as well as the British and French. Arabi said the Egyptians were 'imprisoned, exiled, strangled, thrown into the Nile, starved and robbed according to the will of their masters. The most ignorant Turk was honoured before the best of Egyptians.' He quickly gathered support and was able to force an Egyptian-led military government on Tewfik. How would the French and British take this?

In Paris the French government was faced with troubles of its own. In London, Gladstone was Prime Minister, and he and his ministers thought a display of naval power at Alexandria would make sure that Arabi did what he was told. It was a disastrous decision. When British warships appeared antiforeign feelings flared up. On 11 and 12 June 1882 fifty Europeans were killed in rioting in Alexandria. As one writer has put it, 'In stirring the Egyptian pot, Britain and France had made it boil over.'

Gladstone was in a desperate muddle now. British marines had landed to restore order, and Tewfik took refuge with them. Gladstone, more interested in domestic affairs in England and Ireland, stuck to his idea that total occupation of Egypt would be costly and useless. But Arabi looked very much like a military nationalist adventurer who threatened the enormous sums of money invested there. So, in August of the same year, a small army under Sir Garnet Wolseley landed in Egypt, and within a month defeated Arabi at Tel-el-Kebir.

Sudan Disaster

Having gone unwillingly into Egypt, Gladstone was quite firm on his next move: settle the country's finances and withdraw. One man saw that this would prove impossible—Evelyn Baring. He knew Egypt well, and warned that if Britain left, 'others, probably the French, would take up the work we have failed to do'. Gladstone was unconvinced and gave orders that a withdrawal must occur as soon as possible. Yet soon events to the south of Egypt were to show how little he understood the situation in north-east Africa.

The Sudan, with its vital Upper Nile waters, was also ruled from Cairo, but the annihilation of the Egyptian army at Tel-el-Kebir had encouraged open rebellion. Wandering tribes of cattle-raisers in the west Sudan resented attempts to tax them, and they listened eagerly to the ideas of a religious leader named Muhammad Ahmad. This man, the son of a boat-builder, called for a holy war on all foreigners. In 1881 he proclaimed himself the 'Mahdi', the Saviour of the Muslims. He gradually built up a large following. Discipline was strict. Any Mahdists found drinking wine, which was forbidden, received eighty blows of the kourbash, a vicious rhinoceros-hide whip. His ambition was to weld the various peoples of the Upper Nile into one Sudanese nation, and to set up the Mahdist State, free from any foreign influence.

At first the British took no notice. Then Tewfik sent a small force led by General Hicks to destroy the Mahdi's power. Because of the destruction of the main Egyptian army, this force was poorly equipped and its men were mainly prisoners dragged from the gaols. Hicks wrote in a report, 'We are doomed from the start.' He and his 10,000 men left Cairo in the autumn of 1883 to join up with the few Egyptian outposts still holding out in the Sudan. They were never seen again. For the Mahdi this victory encouraged fresh support for his ambitions.

For Britain it was a disaster which destroyed all Gladstone's plans for a speedy withdrawal from Egypt. Now there was no army at all in the country, except the British. Baring's warning about the French seemed a very real possibility if they left. At the same time Britain had no wish to set about recovering the Sudan—a million square miles of Africa—from the Mahdi. But someone had to be sent to Khartoum to help the men in the remaining Egyptian garrisons get back to Cairo. The choice was General Gordon.

Gordon

Britain was sinking deeper into the quicksand of Egyptian affairs. Worse was to come. Whilst Gordon prepared to move, Gladstone was accused by his colleagues in London of 'abandoning the cause of civilization in the Sudan'. Also Evelyn Baring was worried by the choice of 'Chinese' Gordon, now a popular hero in the minds of many Victorians. Twenty years before in China he had moulded a rabble into a successful fighting force, and had already had considerable experience in the Sudan. Although Gordon welcomed the command, Baring suspected there would be too little glory for the General in merely organizing a quick retreat.

Gordon arrived in Khartoum in February 1884 with secret instructions to evacuate the Egyptian forces. Instead, he set about the task of regaining control of central Sudan. But his force was too small, and by May he had been isolated in the city by the Mahdi. Gladstone was annoyed and for five months shilly-shallied over the expense of sending troops to Gordon's aid. He feared, he said, 'the horrid prospect of asking the British taxpayer to pay for more troops'. Finally, in October, he agreed something must be done. Wolseley, the victor of Tel-el-Kebir, set out from Cairo with a relief expedition, which for three months fought its way up the uncharted Nile against the growing Mahdist power. It arrived forty-eight hours too late, for on 26 January 1885 the Mahdi's army had stormed Khartoum. Gordon died with the defenders.

When the news reached London, the nation mourned a hero. The poet Tennyson, wrote of Gordon:

> Warrior of God, man's friend, not here below,
> But somewhere dead far in the waste Sudan.

Gladstone, who used to be known as G.O.M., the Grand Old Man, was hissed at as M.O.G.—murderer of Gordon. Perhaps though, Gordon's death was his own fault and it was only Victorian propaganda which created the 'hero'. As one historian has written, 'Khartoum was the crown of his life's work. He resented any attempt to make him leave with a passion which suggests that he half-consciously wished to die there!' For Africans the real hero was the Mahdi, who had successfully defied the foreigner.

British Power

British prestige in north-east Africa was very low. Two men were determined to restore it. Evelyn Baring (later to become Lord Cromer) had been appointed as British Consul-General in Egypt in 1883, and he steered the country cautiously back to

February 1885. *Punch* cartoon expresses the fears of Victorian Englishmen for the fate of their hero

prosperity. He was an excellent administrator and he spent his small surpluses of money from taxation on agriculture and railways. He boasted that he was the friend of the peasant because he had banned forced labour and the use of the kourbash.

But Baring made many enemies. He was nicknamed 'Overbearing', for the superior attitude he took when talking to people. Jibes, too, that Egypt was still only a land for foreigners had considerable truth in them. 'Here a palace, where reigns unbridled luxury; there a hovel swarming with people scarcely human', wrote a French visitor about the gap between the standards of living of the ruling class of British, Turks, French and Greeks, and those of the ordinary Egyptians. Cromer never understood that some Egyptians even preferred an inefficient government by their own people to honest, foreign rule!

The other man interested in Britain's reputation abroad was Lord Salisbury, British prime minister for many years at the end of the nineteenth century. He was a master of diplomacy and an imperialist who said that the slogan, 'All British from Cape [South Africa] to Cairo', was a rough statement of his African policy. The Mahdi had died within a year of Gordon's death, and under his successor the Sudan became a wasted land. In ten years its eight million people were steadily reduced, by tribal massacre, famine and disease. Salisbury determined that the Sudan must be reconquered.

A campaign under General Kitchener was launched in 1896. There was to be no repeat of the disasters of the 1880s. As troops moved southwards up the Nile valley a railway was built to secure communications with base. In this way Kitchener made sure he had complete superiority in weapons, equipment and supplies of food. He certainly needed it. His campaign had to deal with cholera and storms as well as the enemy. At Omdurman, just outside Khartoum, battle was joined. On 2 September 1898 Kitchener's Maxim machine guns destroyed the 40,000-strong Dervish army in five hours. Kitchener lost 386 men. The Sudan had been reclaimed.

Fashoda

By 1898 it was obvious that the British intended staying in Egypt and the Sudan. What had started at Cairo in the 1870s as an attempt to secure the Canal route to India, had a quarter

North-east Africa in the colonial era. Boundaries are twentieth century

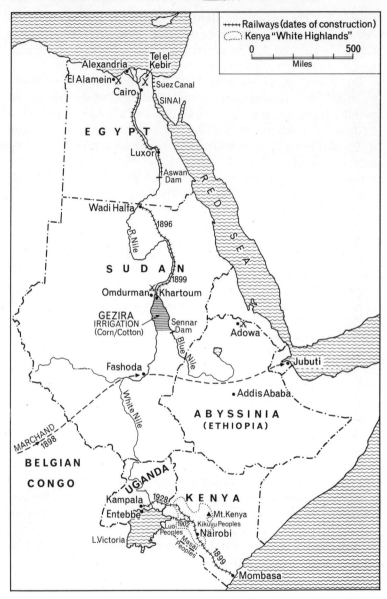

of a century later led the British to seek control of the entire Nile. Now the real threat to British power was France. How real was seen only seventeen days after the Battle of Omdurman.

A French soldier, Captain J. B. Marchand, had been making a hazardous journey from the French Congo across central Africa to the White Nile. The French were determined to stake a claim to some part of the great river. Marchand pitched camp at Fashoda, a hot, swampy place some 300 miles upstream from Khartoum. Kitchener moved swiftly with a small force of soldiers. He met Marchand on 19 September and protested at the French presence. Kitchener had the advantage because Marchand had only eight white men and a few African soldiers.

The British were quite prepared to go to war over the issue, not only in Africa, but in Europe as well. The colonial secretary, Joseph Chamberlain was a very different man from Gladstone. He was even prepared to force a war, 'to trounce France', he said, once for all. But the French climbed down, and Marchand left Fashoda. The River Nile, Egypt and the Sudan were under British control at last, and the route to India secure.

But Britain had to pay a high price for this. Leopold's exploitation of the Congo had only stirred the interest of the nations of Europe in Africa. The steady growth of British control in north-east Africa was another matter. In a kind of chain reaction other European powers had entered a 'scramble' for African territory. Frenchmen were the main rivals to Britain north of the Sahara. In south and central regions it was the Germans, Portuguese and Boers.

Cecil Rhodes had a plan to thwart all of them.

4 Cecil Rhodes–Imperialist

Diamonds

In 1869 some children were found playing with marbles on a farm on the banks of the River Vaal in South Africa. One of these 'marbles' proved to be a superb diamond. This diamond changed the history of South Africa.

Until the 1870s it was a poor, neglected area. There were small white settlements in four places. In two of them, Cape Colony and Natal, lived some British and Boers (descendants of the original Dutch farmers who came to the Cape in the 1650s); the other two were the republics of Transvaal and Orange Free State, founded by Boers who had trekked north in the 1830s to get away from British control at the Cape. None of the four settlements was prosperous.

Within a few years of the diamond discovery 10,000 prospectors arrived. One of them was Cecil John Rhodes, who had earlier come to southern Africa to recover from a tuberculous infection. In one area, later to become the city of Kimberley, six hundred claims were soon being worked by many thousands of people. Rhodes wrote in a letter: 'They have been able to find no bottom yet, and keep on finding steadily at 70 feet. A good claim would average a diamond every load of stuff—a load being about fifty buckets.'

But the great riches of the yellow soil became exhausted. Also the price diamonds fetched on the world's markets tumbled as a result of the sudden flooding with 'stones'. Thousands left Kimberley in despair in the early 1870s. But Rhodes and his friend, Charles Rudd, stayed on, buying up abandoned claims cheaply. They had an instinct that more diamonds were to be found in the blueish ground deep under the previous workings. They were right, and they made their fortunes with the few others who were left like Barnato and Wernher. But the difficulties were enormous. Kimberley was 400 miles from a railway, and there were constant quarrels over the exact boundaries of claims. Rhodes realized that the only efficient answer was

A mass of cables above the Kimberley diamond mine about 1885. Small square claims were mined by individual prospectors who sent their buckets by a cable wire to helpers at the edge of the pit

for the rivals to cooperate, and he persuaded the others to amalgamate with him in 1880 to form the great De Beers Mining Company.

Rhodes's Ambitions

Cecil Rhodes, already a millionaire, also had a taste for power. His work was his life—he was unmarried and had little interest in his own relations. The discovery of gold in Transvaal in 1886 gave him the chance of a second fortune. His money brought him great influence in South Africa, and he rapidly gained political power. By 1890 he was prime minister of Cape Colony.

Rhodes had a complex personality which made him a difficult man to deal with. At times he was hot-tempered, impatient and a hard taskmaster. Some white people found him, however, fair-minded and generous. His ambitions were truly colossal. Sweeping his hand across the map of Africa he would say, 'I would like to see all that red.' He would go on, 'I like the big and the simple, the barbaric if you like. My ruling purpose is the extension of the British Empire.'

In the 1880s Rhodes was not only making money and seeking political power in the Cape. His eyes were also fixed on the north. The dream he wanted to turn into reality was a British-controlled Cape-to-Cairo railway. Lord Salisbury in London distrusted Rhodes, who might upset some of his delicate

25

diplomacy. The British government did not want to provoke trouble with other countries interested in southern Africa— Germany and Portugal as well as the Boer Republics, because Salisbury was doing some difficult bargaining with the European nations about who should control or influence different parts of Africa. Yet Rhodes and Salisbury had this one idea in common: to own a belt of territory running north from the Cape to an area between Portuguese Angola in the west and Mozambique and German East Africa in the east. What was so special about this strip of territory, and where did it lead?

North to Matabeleland and Beyond

Sandwiched between the Kalahari Desert and the Boer Republic of Transvaal was some land through which ran the 'Missionaries' Road' to the north. David Livingstone and Robert Moffat had used this track on their journeys into central Africa. Rhodes in the mid-1880s called it his 'Suez Canal into the interior'. It led to a large, thinly populated plateau, which was quite high and had a climate which Europeans might like. An added attraction were the stories of gold which filtered into South Africa from returning hunters and missionaries.

The Boers in Transvaal were also known to be interested. Some years before Rhodes had warned the Cape Parliament. 'Shall we allow these petty republics,' he said angrily, 'to form a wall across our trade route?' No one, however, was prepared to support him until the Germans began showing colonial ambitions in 1885. Later the British government in London gave Rhodes permission to send a small force—a pioneer column it was called—to take control of the route and the plateau.

Before it could move one danger had to be dealt with: the kingdom of the Matabele, one of the most formidable peoples in southern Africa, and an offshoot of the Zulu nation. The Matabele, warriors and cattle-keepers, were ruled by a king and council, and their attitude to foreigners, black or white was often hostile. To them all cattle were their property and all peoples their lawful victims. For the Matabele were a military nation and to their way of thinking, war and hunting were proper occupations for men.

Earlier, in 1870, Lobengula had become king of the Matabele. He was a man of outstanding ability, intelligent and a fine administrator. Descriptions of Lobengula vary, and come from Europeans only. Those who saw him as a barrier to their ambitions called him 'a gross, fat man with a cruel restless eye'. Others, like a French explorer with no particular interest in southern Africa, called him 'an imposing monarch'. His six-foot height gave him 'a most majestic appearance'. He controlled a compact area around his capital, Bulawayo, and in each of the forty settlements within a radius of thirty miles of it was a regiment of soldiers. Lobengula could quickly call on a force of 20,000 men eager to defend their nation. He was clearly a dangerous foe, despite his declaration that all he wished for was to be left in peace with his cattle, his beer and his sixty-eight wives.

It was a vain hope for Lobengula. He faced difficult problems: he was challenged in his authority by rival Matabele aristocrats, and he was plagued by Europeans wanting to dig for gold. He grew restless. White men, he said, were coming into his territory 'like wolves'. On one thing he was firm: 'I want no Boers. They stole my father's country.' Only two generations previously his peoples had retreated north from the Vaal River area after clashing with Boers. But Lobengula said he believed that the 'great White Queen' (Victoria) was trustworthy, so in 1888 he agreed to meet the British. Rhodes sent Charles Rudd immediately to Bulawayo to obtain permission to seek gold. The meeting set in motion a train of events which led to the formation of a new white-dominated country in central Africa.

The Founding of Rhodesia

On 30 October 1888 Rudd persuaded Lobengula to grant to Rhodes 'complete and exclusive charge over all metals and minerals in my kingdom . . . with full permission to do all things necessary to win and procure the same'. For this concession Lobengula would receive £100 a month, one thousand rifles and a gunboat for the Zambezi River. Rhodes acted quickly. Within weeks he was in London forming a company to develop the mines—the British South Africa Company. Soon it was backed by wealthy business men hoping for more diamond or gold discoveries.

Did Lobengula realize what he was doing? The gold area was thought to be to the north and east of Matabeleland. Here

The founding of Rhodesia 1890. The southern area also shows the clash of British, Boer and African territorial ambitions

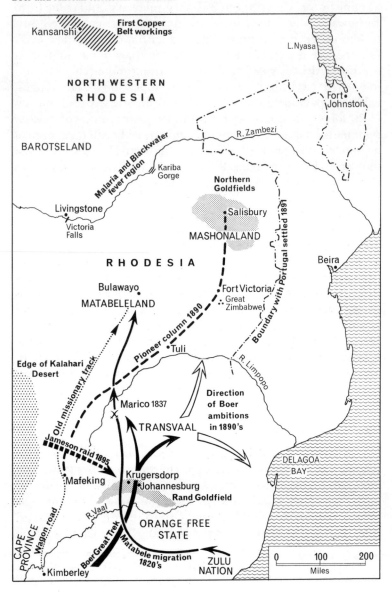

lived the Shona peoples, craftsmen and traders, much despised by their overlords, the Matabele. Perhaps Lobengula hoped the Rudd Concession would get rid of the white men who were pestering him in Bulawayo. Anyway he remarked that he did not think more than a dozen men would come and dig. And he wanted those rifles!

Rhodes was not thinking on these lines at all. With Lobengula's signature he set about persuading the British government in London to allow his new company to *govern* the area. This was illegal as the Lobengula agreement made no mention of political control, but Lord Salisbury knew that if he did not grant this the Boers in Transvaal might seize the place. Within a year Rhodes was given all he wanted in a Royal Charter. Besides controlling the trade, he could make treaties and laws, and build up a police force to enforce them. These were enormous powers—almost those of a nation state. The British South Africa Company's prospects now looked so good that investors rushed to buy shares. *The Times* in London wrote of 'a land three times the size of the United Kingdom, a land of milk and honey, gold and diamonds'.

Rhodes had achieved one of his great ambitions. He was only thirty-six years old. But there were plenty of dangers and problems ahead. The plateau had to be reached and settled. Soon Lobengula would realize that he had been hoodwinked. Would the Matabele accept the Charter without a fight?

At last, in June 1890, the Pioneer Column of 117 wagons moved north. In it were 200 settlers who went with the promise of gold claims and 3,000 acres of land each; also 200 police went at five shillings a day to keep law and order. The Column's destination was Mashonaland, but it had to pass dangerously close to Bulawayo. The going was slow—ten miles a day. A road had to be cut, and continuous patrolling was necessary for fear of a Matabele attack. Small forts were built at regular intervals so that some sort of permanent communication would be kept with the Cape. By September the 400 mile journey was complete and no lives had been lost. Lobengula had honoured his side of the bargain. The Union Jack was hoisted over a final, rapidly constructed, fort, named Salisbury, after the British prime minister.

The Column disbanded and scattered over the sparsely

populated country to open up farms and gold claims. Life seemed free and easy, and full of promise, until the rains came in November 1890. Then tent life became primitive and uncomfortable, especially when the only road, southwards to the outside world, was flooded. Prices of food rose sharply: butter was 11s. a pound, beer 6s. 6d. a pint, and paraffin £2 a gallon. Rhodes tried to get money for a railway. 'I cannot feed them by the overland route', he wrote to Lord Salisbury. 'I must have a railway. I do not want, next year, 10,000 people shut up like rats in a trap.' For the Pioneer Column had brought many others to Mashonaland in its wake. Rhodes got his way, although it took six years to build. Meanwhile, things improved. Brick houses, schools and a hospital were built.

Through these early years, in what some called Zambezia and others Rhodesia, Lobengula kept his warriors quiet. He knew the alternative to Rhodes was occupation by the Transvaal Boers. But his trust turned to suspicion; the growing strength of the Company worried and angered him. He was under pressure from leading Matabele who knew Rhodes had tricked them, so Lobengula allowed his soldiers to steal cattle and cut telegraph wires. Equally ill-feeling arose amongst the settlers. They determined to deal with Lobengula. They were disappointed that their gold claims had produced so little. And rumours grew that perhaps there was some near Bulawayo. So, equipped with machine guns, two thousand settlers marched on Lobengula's capital.

Lobengula was furious. 'The white men are fathers of liars,' he cried. Daubed with paint in the old Zulu fashion, 12,000 Matabele came out to do battle in September 1893. The war was brief. As Rhodes had foreseen, the Matabele had no idea how to use the rifles sent to him under the Rudd agreement. Lobengula, that 'naked, old savage' as Rhodes called him, died, and his warriors were massacred with superior weapons. Rhodes justified the war by referring to the Matabele as 'the last, ruthless power of barbarism that existed in South Africa'. Yet there was little honourable in this annihilation of the Matabele kingdom, for the Rudd Concession had been gained under false pretences, and it was Lobengula who had kept his word as the Pioneer Column moved northwards.

For the Matabele their tragedy was supreme. Their nation

Wagons of the pioneer column to Mashonaland preparing to cross a river

lay in ruins because of the clash between, says one historian, 'Rhodes wielding the armed might and financial power of the Cape and Britain, and Lobengula ruling a fighting nation which happened to occupy an area rich in gold and favoured with land suitable for white settlement.'

Matabeleland was occupied by settlers and Bulawayo became a thriving white town of 2,000 people. But the Matabele and even the Shona rebelled again in 1896. They fought the white man for over a year against great odds, yet their defeat was inevitable against the modern arms of the settlers. For many years bitterness lingered in Rhodesia. White and black had come into violent collision, and race relations were badly affected well into the twentieth century.

In 1894 Rhodes stood at the highest point of success. His ambitions knew no limit. 'I have a greater and bigger idea,' he said in that year, 'and that is the union of all South Africa.' The Boers had other ideas.

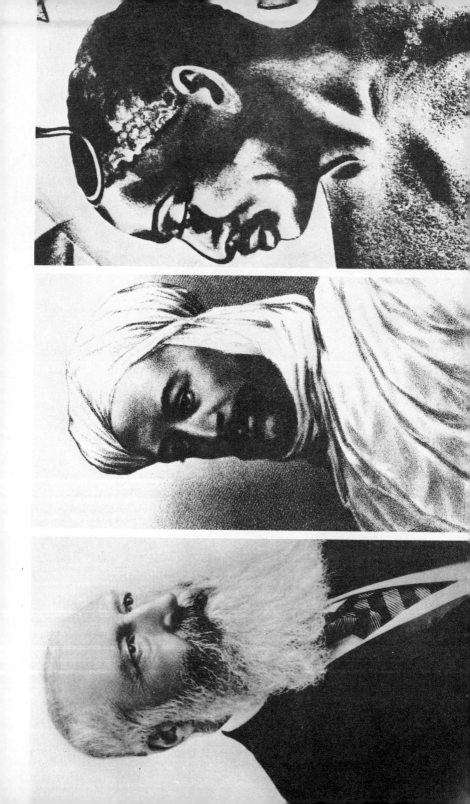

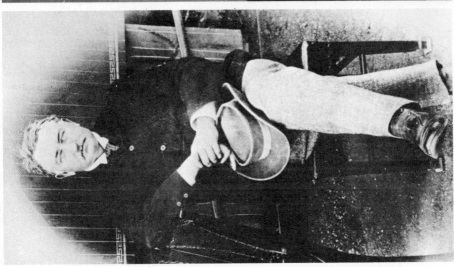

Above left: Leopold, King of the Belgians and ruler of the Congo Free State

Above centre: The Mahdi, ruler of the Sudan in the mid-1880s

Above right: Lobengula, King of the Matabele

Right: Cecil John Rhodes, millionaire, Cape Premier, empire-builder

Far right: Paulus Kruger, president of Transvaal Republic

5 The Struggle between Briton and Boer

'Oom Paul' Kruger

In the South African city of Pretoria today stands a piece of massive granite. On it is a statue cast in bronze of Paulus Kruger, one of the most remarkable men in South Africa in the last part of the nineteenth century. The metal cast gives a clue to his character: broad shoulders hunched forward; a stubborn chin sunk in a straggly beard; small eyes and pouched eyelids set wide apart in a heavy, unsmiling face.

Kruger was President of Transvaal Republic, and is today thought of as the 'father' of Afrikaner or Boer nationalism. Aged ten, he left the British-ruled Cape Colony to trek northwards with his father, a poor sheep-farmer. Many other Boers (a Dutch word for 'farmer') did the same, and in the 1850s two separate and independent countries, Transvaal and Orange Free State were set up. But the small and struggling farming communities had many difficulties. They were constantly quarrelling, both amongst themselves and with the African tribes who spread out like a great horseshoe around the northern end of the Boer territories. Kruger slowly climbed to power. When the Boer communities north of the River Vaal merged into a single republic, he became commander of the various Boer 'commando' units which frequently had to fight African tribes who stole their cattle. This was a costly business, and Transvaal's budget was always in difficulties. In 1883 Kruger was elected President, an office which he held for the next seventeen years.

Kruger became 'Oom Paul' (meaning 'uncle', a term of respect for elders) to the Boers, and he saw himself as the new Moses, leading his people into the promised land. He was admired for his courage, iron will, his leadership of men, and, in particular, for his stand against the ruthlessness of men like Rhodes. He had a sharp intelligence, but he was suspicious of foreigners and found it difficult to see the other person's point of view. Unfortunately for the future of southern Africa,

Kruger's obstinacy was well matched by three Englishmen who also took a major part in the story of the area in the 1890s: Cecil Rhodes (Cape premier), Joseph Chamberlain (British colonial secretary) and Alfred Milner (British high commissioner in Cape Town).

Gold and the Rand

In 1886 gold was discovered in central Transvaal. The rush that followed created Johannesburg, today the biggest city in Africa after Cairo. It grew up above part of the reef of gold ore which runs across Transvaal for a hundred miles or so and goes down a mile deep. The centre of the mining became known as the Rand, short for Witwatersrand or Ridge of White Waters. Most of the gold prospectors were British, who brought the money, equipment and experience needed for the deep mining operations.

The taxes which Kruger put on the gold miners saved the Transvaal from bankruptcy. In 1886 the entire revenue of the republic was only £200,000; in 1896 it was £4 million. However, the Boers were appalled by the rabble of foreigners ('Uitlanders', they called them), who came to Johannesburg. Kruger had fears for the future. 'It is my country they want', he declared.

Some Boers, like the young Jan Smuts, hoped for some kind of federation, in which the British and Boers linked their future together in a great United States of South Africa. Rhodes also had thought this was possible in the early days, but he did not trust Kruger. Transvaal, with its gold, possessed such a vast treasure-house that the lesson was clear. Whoever rules Transvaal will, in the end, control southern Africa.

It was rumoured in Britain that Kruger believed God's will would make the Afrikaner-Boer master in South Africa. To this end he would refuse any non-Boer, white or black, a voice in the running of his country. Neither Rhodes nor the British government was prepared to accept this fate. So, by the mid-1890s, a contest for the domination of Africa south of the Zambezi had begun between Briton and Boer. Rhodes thought he had a simple answer. 'The best way,' he said, 'of checking the expansion of the Boer Republic is to enclose it.' By establishing Rhodesia he was already three-quarters towards achieving this.

35

But the route to one piece of territory still lay open—Delagoa Bay, near the mouth of the Limpopo River, a natural outlet for the Boers to the Indian Ocean. Here the Portuguese had a small settlement and the British feared that Transvaal might buy it or take it from Portugal. The Germans too had shown interest here, and the British in London were very suspicious of any other European power with ambitions in South Africa.

The Jameson Raid

Efforts were made in London to ensure that the Boers could not secure Delagoa Bay. They failed. Rhodes, who was now in poor health, grew more impatient, for Kruger's power was growing.

Inside the Transvaal the Uitlanders became disgruntled at their treatment by the Boers. Kruger's 'Hollanders', as they called them, were greedy and corrupt. Not only were normal taxes high, but the mining businesses had to pay extortionate prices for dynamite. Also the mining community formed an expanding force. By 1895 the Boers, who were scattered in small farms all over the country, were nearly outnumbered by the 80,000 Uitlanders in Johannesburg. Yet Kruger offered to give these 'baboons in my backyard' only very limited political rights. He was probably correct in thinking that if he granted equality, Boer control in Transvaal would soon end, but he made a bad mistake in treating the Uitlanders like second-class citizens, and calling them 'thieves'.

In 1895 a Uitlander rebellion was being discussed. Rhodes supported this, but his planning and choice of leader, Dr Jameson, for a Cape force to help the Uitlanders was disastrous. The plot was muddled and so badly was the secret kept that the Boers knew all about it. However, Jameson, who was supposed to wait with his small force at the Cape-Transvaal border until the Uitlanders actually rebelled, saw himself as a modern Clive of India. 'Anyone could take Transvaal with half-a-dozen revolvers,' he boasted. Unknown to Jameson feelings in Johannesburg were changing. The miners and clerks were losing interest in rebellion because a new gold boom came to the Rand late in 1895.

Jameson, anyway, had decided to act on his own. Rhodes told him not to move too early, but this advice was ignored. With 356 men Jameson crossed into Transvaal in the last week of December, declaring he would drive the Boers into the sea. He himself knew little of war and the discipline of his force was poor. At one point he ordered some telegraph wires to be cut, but the man detailed for the job was so drunk that he cut and buried wires from a farmer's fence instead! The Raid proved a fiasco, and Jameson's men were halted at Krugersdorp. One of them recorded: 'At nine-fifteen on 2 January 1896 someone hoisted a white cloth. Jameson, seeing the sign of surrender, fell over as if shot.'

The Raid widened the rift between Briton and Boer. Even moderate Boers now threw their hand in with Kruger, for it seemed that British imperialism had aimed a blow at Afrikaner independence. The real issue became clear. It was not about routes to the sea, or dynamite prices, or Uitlanders voting rights. The British High Commissioner in Cape Town, Alfred Milner, put it bluntly when he talked of the 'great power game between ourselves and the Transvaal for mastery in South Africa'.

The Raid also destroyed Rhodes's career as prime minister of Cape Colony, because the final responsibility for failure was his. But in London others were involved, and they were impatient for a showdown with Kruger.

War: the British miscalculate

Joseph Chamberlain was probably at that time the ablest man in English politics. In Lord Salisbury's government he had chosen his own position—colonial secretary. Although he was sixty years old he felt his drive and energy could be used to advance British imperialism. 'Our race,' he declared in a Birmingham speech, 'is the greatest of all governing races.' Many people thought he was a dangerous man who would cause unnecessary trouble abroad. They called this tall, elegant figure with a monocle and orchid button-hole 'Pushful Joe'.

On South Africa Chamberlain and Alfred Milner were in agreement. The country must be firmly in British hands. Chamberlain told Milner to negotiate for better rights for the Uitlanders in Transvaal, but all the meetings failed. Kruger's position may be summarized: 'This is my country, these are my laws. If you do not like them you may leave my country.' Chamberlain complained angrily that 'Mr Kruger dribbles out reforms like water from a squeezed sponge'. Milner too

Punch cartoon of March 1900 shows that some people realized very early on that the Boers would never accept permanent British domination in South Africa

A HANDSOME OFFER:

BOER (*considerably damaged*). "I DIDN'T LIKE TO MENTION IT BEFORE, BUT NOW THAT 'YOU 'VE RECOVERED YOUR PRESTIGE,' GIVE ME EVERYTHING I WANT AND ALL SHALL BE FORGIVEN !"

soon lost faith in negotiation. The feeling spread in British South Africa that Kruger would not yield until 'he looked down a cannon's mouth'.

In fact both sides were preparing for war. The contest would be an uneven one, and final British victory was inevitable considering British military, naval and industrial power. However,

Chamberlain and Milner made some tragic miscalculations. They thought a military solution would be a 'rapid and pain-less operation'. Yet the British had to put half a million troops in the field to defeat the Boers' 50,000 strong force. The war which broke out in October 1899 was long and costly. The Boer armies and guerrilla groups called commandos fought with courage and tenacity for nearly three years. Casualties on both sides were high and destruction widespread when peace was finally signed in 1902.

As soon as the war was over some Boer statesmen like Smuts tried to work with the British, and detailed arrangements were made for a unified South Africa to receive its independence in 1910. Here again the British miscalculated. They thought that the war had solved everything. Kruger's nationalism was crush-ed, and the new, independent Union of South Africa would be pro-British like Canada and Australia.

Yet for many Boers the war had merely intensified their bitterness towards the British. Women and children had been crowded into 'concentration camps' and had had their homes burnt in order to cut off food supplies to the Boer commandos. Defeat did not change their old Afrikaner attitudes. They still believed in the idea of 'wit baasskap', which means literally, 'white-man-boss'. Because of this the Boers loathed British efforts after the war to bring Black Africans and even Chinese labour into the cities to help recovery from the devastation. In any case many Boers thought the British were two-faced. With Chamberlain's 'Our Race' speech in mind, they said the war had been fought not to give equal rights and opportunities to Black Africans, but merely to replace Boer control by British control.

The British military victory was to prove a hollow one. Paulus Kruger died in lonely exile in Switzerland in 1904, but his Boer-Afrikaner followers in Transvaal were later to revive the struggle against British domination. We shall see how it worked out in chapter 20.

6 Why the Scramble?

The Chain of Events

European governments partitioned most of Africa amongst themselves in the period 1884–1902. Probably the first links in this chain of events were the activities of Leopold in the Congo and of the British in Egypt. In the African situation just prior to this two points are worth noting.

First, Britain and France were the only two west European nations with enough political and economic power to interest themselves overseas. Until the 1860s neither Germany nor Italy existed as separate states. Small countries like Holland had given up or lost their African possessions, and Portugal was looked upon as a very minor competitor.

Secondly, trade between Europeans and Africans was largely restricted to coastal regions. Most of this trade, too, was free to all-comers, which suited Britain because her industrial goods were greater in quantity and better in quality than her competitors. She could sell sufficient goods in these areas to make it unnecessary to venture farther inland. In any case she had a flourishing trade with North and Latin America, Australia, India and the East. Nor did Britain want to colonize, for, as Disraeli said, 'Colonies are a millstone round our neck'.

In the 1870s and early 1880s the situation changed. Trade then was no longer coastal. The occasional railway and river steamship took rival traders deep into the interior, and to prevent any clashes Britain and France began thinking in terms of 'spheres of influence', areas in which each country would have the monopoly of trade.

At this point two new 'powers' showed interest in Africa. The first was Leopold, whose ambitions we have seen centred on the rubber and ivory trade of the Congo basin. This worried a French trading company with interests on the northern bank of the river. Its agent, de Brazza, had the support of his home government and the company soon extended its activities round the coast to the mouth of the Niger River, thus avoiding conflict with Leopold. But this move, in turn, touched British trading at a sensitive spot—the mouth of the Niger, where George Goldie had been efficiently establishing British control over local African rulers. Leopold had now created an atmosphere of suspicion between the Europeans with trading interests in west and central Africa.

The nation which converted this suspicious rivalry into a feverish scramble for African territory was Germany, the new power in European politics. United in 1871, after the Prussian defeat of Austria and France, its industrial strength was increasing rapidly, and its ruler, Bismarck, was a formidable diplomat. The 'birthday' of Germany's colonial empire in Africa came in 1884. Until then Bismarck had declared he was uninterested in overseas territories. He quickly changed his ideas when he realized that German prestige in Europe could be increased by acquiring colonies, most easily in Africa. Here he could use his diplomatic skill to play the British off against the French. On 24 April, Germany declared South-west Africa to be a protectorate; within twelve months German explorers enabled Bismarck to lay claim to three other widely separated areas: Togoland, Cameroons and in East Africa.

Immediately Bismarck showed how important German power in Africa was. As we have seen, Britain was involved in Egyptian finances and government. Bismarck assured Britain of German bankers' support there on condition she did not block German expansion elsewhere. This was especially important in East Africa, where Karl Peters had in ten days persuaded twelve African chieftains to accept German control of 60,000 square miles. As one writer says, Peters managed this 'by a judicious distribution of toys, plus an injudicious application of grog!'

The scramble for territory had now begun in earnest, and in 1884–85 fourteen European countries met at Berlin to establish some kind of international rule. Here Leopold gained recognition of his right to rule the Congo basin, and the Congo and Niger Rivers were declared free to all traders. Also a simple rule was laid down: any power could acquire African lands by 'effectively occupying' them. In the next six years most of Africa was claimed by occupying a coastal region, and then defining the boundaries by running a line inland on a map. This

The futility of resistance. An African artist in this bas-relief from Abomey, west Africa, shows the superiority of white man's armaments

has been called the 'Paper Partition' of Africa, when the European nations agreed amongst themselves where the main lines of control should run. It was remarkably bloodless. But it was only the start. Later violence became savage and prolonged.

In the 1890s partition 'on the ground' followed when coastal control was extended inland. Inevitably collisions occurred, both amongst European military expeditions and with the more powerful African peoples.

Leopold's agents destroyed Arab control in the Upper Congo; the British and French nearly went to war at Fashoda; and white fought white for supremacy in South Africa. But African resistance to loss of sovereignty was fierce in places. We have seen how the Matabele empire fought the Rhodesian settlers, and noted the success and failure of the Mahdist state against Anglo-Egyptian pressure. The map on page 43 shows the extent of other African opposition throughout the continent. In East Africa (today's southern Tanzania) 200,000 lost their lives in the Maji-Maji Rebellion against German occupation, and an equal number died in the fifteen-year resistance to the French invasion of West Africa. After subduing Morocco, the French moved across the Sahara to the Upper Niger, and fought the well-organized Ivory Coast peoples and the empire of Samori Touré. In the long run African victory was rare, but

Examples of African resistance to European colonial rule before 1939

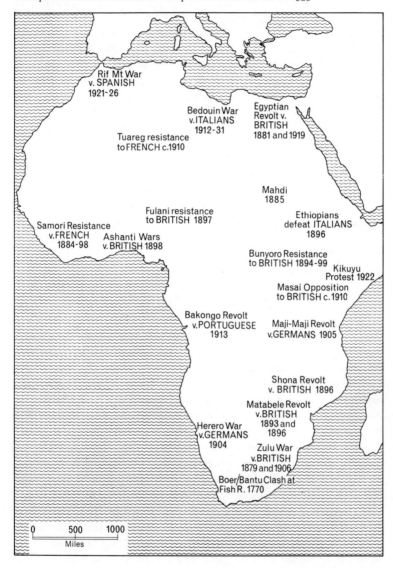

Rif Mt War
v. SPANISH
1921-26

Bedouin War
v. ITALIANS
1912-31

Egyptian
Revolt v.
BRITISH
1881 and 1919

Tuareg resistance
to FRENCH c.1910

Mahdi
1885

Fulani resistance
to BRITISH 1897

Ethiopians
defeat ITALIANS
1896

Samori Resistance
v. FRENCH
1884-98

Ashanti Wars
v. BRITISH 1898

Bunyoro Resistance
to BRITISH 1894-99

Kikuyu
Protest 1922

Masai Opposition
to BRITISH c.1910

Bakongo Revolt
v. PORTUGUESE
1913

Maji-Maji Revolt
v. GERMANS 1905

Shona Revolt
v. BRITISH 1896

Matabele Revolt
v. BRITISH
1893 and
1896

Herero War
v. GERMANS
1904

Zulu War
v. BRITISH
1879 and 1906

Boer/Bantu Clash at
Fish R. 1770

0   500   1000
Miles

43

they gained some signal successes. The Zulu nation imposed perhaps the greatest defeat of British arms in colonial history at Isandhlwana in 1879; and at Adowa in 1896 the Emperor Menelek shattered Italian forces trying to seize Abyssinia.

Thus, in 1870 more than 90 per cent of Africa was ruled by its own inhabitants. At the beginning of the twentieth century all but a small fraction was governed by Europeans.

Why?

There is no single explanation that would account for the remarkable and ruthless sequence of events in the scramble for Africa. Duty and love of adventure were reasons which appealed to contemporaries. Newspapers gave front page coverage to far-off successes. The stirring stories of Rider Haggard sold well, and the verse of Rudyard Kipling went down well with Victorian consciences.

> Take up the White Man's Burden—
> Send for the best ye breed . . .

But these explanations were mainly afterthoughts. Not until very late on did men like Rhodes and Chamberlain show any interest in the 'romantic glories of ruling desert and bush'.

Perhaps there is some truth in what are called 'economic' arguments. European industry and prosperity saw Africa in two ways: as a source of raw materials and as a market for products. So the partition of Africa was encouraged by importers of rubber, raw cotton, coffee, copra, by exporters of calico (a coarse, printed cotton cloth), cheap alcohol, armaments, railway and telegraph materials, and by merchants and bankers. In the early twentieth century enemies of the 'imperialists', like the Russian Lenin, made much of this. He argued that Europe's rich industrialists had so much money to spare ('capital') that they had to look overseas for likely places to invest it. Only then could this surplus capital earn more money for the capitalists. This economic argument seemed to provide a neat answer. But the detailed description in the last six chapters shows that in many cases these men did not 'cause' the partition. They merely throve on it.

What then is the solution? Why did the scramble take place?

The answer lies in a combination of two forces, one from outside and one from inside Africa.

The first force was a kind of nationalism, the seeking of national prestige which followed the creation of a powerful German Empire and a united Italy. A German explorer in 1881 insisted that 'through imperialistic efforts a country exhibits before the world its strength or weakness as a nation'. A year later the French premier echoed this. If France stayed out of the search for colonies she would, he said, 'descend from the first rank to the third or fourth'.

This argument explains why the situation in the mid-1880s differed from that of 1870. Germany was a rising power, France a declining one. Both looked to Africa to improve their position. However, to explain why Britain acquired her African empire is

The Maxim gun being tested by Edward, Prince of Wales at Wimbledon 1888. Ernest Maxim, the inventor, looks on

more complicated. For generations London governments had sought to preserve a balance of power in Britain's relations with the rest of the world. So, if a European country became interested in a part of Africa which somehow threatened Britain's security or trade, then her statesmen felt obliged to step in—to 'redress the balance' it was called. Here then was the second force: events inside Africa. The keys to the scramble as far as Britain was concerned lay in Egypt and the Transvaal. The story of the crises here has been told.

It is clear that around 1870 Britain's wealth, naval power and industrial supremacy gave her great influence in Africa's coastal regions. Three things, Bismarck's diplomacy, Ismail's bankruptcy and Kruger's ambitions for his Boers threatened in different ways to destroy this heritage. By 1900 men like Salisbury, Chamberlain, Rhodes, Cromer and Lugard had attempted to revitalize British influence. On a map their efforts looked highly successful. An impressive area of Africa was under British control at the end of the scramble.

It might be thought that the British, with the French, Germans and Portuguese would now set about modernizing their new possessions. But nothing of the kind happened. For Africa was partitioned not for present needs, but as a form of 'insurance' for the future. Also this partition took place with hardly any reference to Africans. In the minds of Europeans, African wishes simply did not count. Why in most cases were they overwhelmed so easily? An Englishman put it in verse:

> Whatever happens we have got
> The Maxim Gun, and they have not.

7 Africa as seen by Colonial Officials and Settlers

Too Much to Do, Too Little Money

The scramble for Africa had created large areas which Europeans must now govern. Some questions had to be faced immediately. How was a colony to be administered—directly by the home government from its European capital, or was there to be some local control? Who were to be the men-on-the-spot, and how many of these 'officials' should there be? Who was to meet the cost—the European taxpayer? Also some obvious improvements must take place: trade and sound government need efficient communications, so harbours, railways and roads had to be built. But the speed of partition and the fact that Africa was wanted mainly as a safeguard for the future rather than immediate development meant that no colonial power was prepared to pay heavily to solve even some of these urgent African problems.

The ideal colony from the point of view of London, Paris, Brussels or Berlin was one which was self-supporting. Once possession was agreed and recognized then European governments felt their sole duty to Africa was keeping law and order. They had grave problems of their own. Industrial unrest, a costly arms race, the First World War, the Great Depression— all these took European attention away from Africa in the first thirty years of the twentieth century.

The real burden of ruling Africa thus fell on a few administrators. For instance, Sir Harry Johnston was sent to Nyasaland with £10,000 a year. On this he found he could afford a 'police force' of seventy-five Indian soldiers and one British officer for a country longer north to south than England. Another man, Frederick Lugard, went to keep law and order in northern Nigeria, where powerful Muslim rulers had much influence over its ten million people. For this task he had a mere £100,000, five officials and a single regiment of 2,500 soldiers.

European ignorance of African conditions led to great difficulties. In West Africa no one knew the cause of malaria, yellow

Passengers being rowed to waiting ships off the Liberian coast in the early colonial period. The African coastline has few natural harbours and artificial ones were very costly

fever or sleeping sickness. Little was known of the natural resources apart from some cocoa, gold and palm oil. Transport was a nightmare. Sandbars and rapids made movement by river difficult, and in the rain forest belt head-loads were the only way of carrying goods. Here animal transport was impossible because the tsetse fly weakened or killed haulage beasts. The hundreds of local languages and customs added to the difficulties of the few trained officials. Administration, health, education, forestry and communication had to be tackled with scanty resources.

The African coastline has few good natural harbours. Freetown was the only one in West Africa. So the French decided they must create one—at Dakar. But the dredging of this magnificent manmade harbour took most of the local revenue for many years. To get inland cheap one-track railways were built, and later some feeder-roads were laid to the railheads. It was a slow process. In the Gold Coast it took three years to construct a railway from Sekondi to Tarkwa, forty miles inland. Eventually the line was extended to Kumasi, a further hundred miles. Although the colonial governments were desperately short of capital, the benefits to be had from improving communications were obvious. A head-load from the coast to Kumasi cost 26s. 6d.; by rail it cost 4s.

These examples from West Africa could be multiplied many

times over the continent as a whole. And considering its enormous size such small scale activities were only scratching the surface of the problem of modernizing Africa.

Two Different Theories

Each colonial power worked out its own ideas on government. The French and British ideas for example were quite different.

The French were conscious of a mission to bring civilization to Africa. In their language the verb 'assimiler' means 'to cause to resemble'. So French colonial policy was called 'assimilation'. It assumed that what was good for the French nation was good for other nations, and the peoples of Africa were to be turned into Frenchmen—speaking, living, behaving and thinking like Frenchmen. It had distinct advantages. In theory the colonies were centrally administered so an official in the overseas service could easily be posted.

Africans were offered French citizenship once they accepted a European way of life. But up to the Second World War only about 3,000 applied for such citizenship out of the French colonial population of 20 million. Devout Muslims objected to several of the conditions laid down. They had to become Christians, give up polygamy and have their children educated in the French language. Merchants, too, thought the trading arrangements were very one-sided. They were forced to buy and sell in French markets, yet when British Gold Coast cocoa was cheaper than that of the French Ivory Coast, Paris dealers went to Accra!

For the British, Lugard, successful in Nigeria, in 1922 laid out his theories in a book, *The Dual Mandate in Tropical Africa*. It became a sort of handbook for British colonial officials elsewhere in Africa. It argued that indirect rule (the opposite of French theory) worked the best. In this version of local government, the African chieftain was the key. He was responsible to a British official, such as the District Officer, but the chief had his own agents, who presided over the courts administering African justice, and collecting taxes which were divided between local and colonial needs. Lugard's ideas worked well with the Muslim emirs of northern Nigeria, and this area became the showpiece of indirect rule.

Like 'assimilation' it had its weaknesses. Not all African

Portuguese
British
French
Belgian
German
Spanish
Italian

0   500   1000
Miles

peoples had chiefs, and anyway, many chiefs had lost their prestige and authority over the people during the 'scramble' period. The British thought their ideas had one special advantage over the French. Britain said she was only a 'trustee' for her colonies. When trained and modernized these colonies would become self-governing, although this was expected to be a long time in the future—so long in fact that educated Africans wondered about the reliability of British promises. France felt no such obligation. She would share the benefits of civilization, but the relationship was clearly that of father and son, and the son was not allowed to grow up too quickly.

The Men-on-the-spot

By 1914 the number of European officials in each colony had grown from the original few to some hundreds. Military control had given way to civilians, and under the Governor were provincial and district officers. The District Officer has been called the 'lynch-pin of the whole system'. At the start he was usually an ex-army officer or big-game hunter who knew the area. Then the British began recruiting their D.O.s from the universities, but a 1930 Report on the Colonial Service listed a university degree as only one of the qualifications needed; the others were, 'vision, high ideals of service, fearless devotion to duty, tolerance and, above all, team spirit'.

A District Officer's task was a difficult one. One day he might have to call on an African merchant in Lagos, a rich, well-respected figure who had sat with the Governor a few days ago at the race-course. A dignified, courteous host, the merchant would discuss English politics, and how his son was doing at Cambridge University. The interior of the house was so 'European' that the D.O. might well note in his diary, 'It was with a shock of surprise that I noticed the family photographs were of black people.' Another D.O. could be 700 miles to the north, in a community almost cut off from the rest of the world. Here he might learn of traditional cannibalism. A senior head of the household, when he succeeded to the position, had 'the heart of his predecessor served up to him in a human skull. He ate solemnly, that the power of the dead might live on in him. He refreshes this power by eating human flesh from time to time.'

Some District Officers found it difficult to adapt to such a variety of standards. It was all too easy in some areas to sit back and give orders, and remind the chief that his position (and salary) depended on the D.O. and that glowing report he was about to write to the Governor! The chief was then left to do the unpopular work of collecting a heavy tax, or allocating 'voluntary' labour to repair a road washed away in the rains.

However, these men-on-the-spot were often the agents of all that was best in colonial rule. They supervised native courts, experimental farms, leper settlements, maternity clinics and anti-locust operations. These were the men who, with the chiefs, organized the clearing of the flybush. In one operation in Tanganyika in 1930, 15,000 men armed with axes and knives were let loose on the bush on a front eight miles long. They worked for ten-day periods. Three years later sixty square miles had been cleared for farming.

Settlers

Not all Britons supported Lugard's ideas. In 1924 Lord Leverhulme declared: 'The African native will be happier and produce the best when his labour is directed and organized by his white brother, who has all these million years start ahead of him.'

White settlers from Britain and the European continent were already established in South Africa and on the Algerian coast; now they came in their thousands to the Kenya Highlands, Southern Rhodesia and Madagascar, and in their hundreds to the Portuguese and ex-German colonies, where crop plantations were established. Colonial governments who were short of money encouraged these settlements because they employed Africans on the farms and these could then pay taxes.

Though few in number, white settlers formed an energetic, prosperous and powerful group. A settler's dream was to turn his little piece of Africa into something like his home country. The end product of this hard work was often very pleasant. One writer describes a Kenyan settler's day:

'In the morning the farmer would be out at dawn, the air raw, smoke from the African huts lying in a blue haze round the wet thatch. He would get the work of the farm started, and perhaps ride round the gangs at work before breakfast. In the middle of the morning the sun would be warm enough to walk about without a sweater, the heat would bring out the smell of red dust and the rising tang of cypress. There would be the thump of a tractor working, the lowing of cattle and the sharp cry of a circling buzzard. By mid-afternoon most of the work would be finished and the farm silent and sleepy with heat. As the sun went down the air would chill with a hint of frost, and the farmer would sprawl before a roaring log-fire in a great stone fire-place, the room littered with dogs, cats, vases of flowers and the old and well-loved furniture.'

Verdict

Officials, settlers and European governments assumed that colonial rule would last for hundreds of years. Events were to prove them wrong. Yet their achievements were many: peace, modern communications, machinery and schools. The Ghanaian, Kofi Busia, has written: 'The most remarkable contribution of colonialism in Africa was in ideas and techniques—the ideas of justice, freedom of speech, worship and travel, the rule of law, and the techniques of voting and administration.'

How a European measures the balance sheet of loss and gain of colonial rule depends probably on who he is: government minister, ex-district officer, settler, trader or missionary. Perhaps a contemporary remark by the distinguished and sympathetic writer on African affairs, Margery Perham, makes the point clearly. In 1931 she wrote of the colonial rulers: 'We are like a man who, in striding through a wood, puts his foot through a beautiful cobweb, and, turning in regret, tries to reconstruct it.'

One thing was certain. The cobweb of the old African way of life was broken for ever. Some Africans welcomed change; others were not so sure.

53

8 African Viewpoints

First Thoughts and Mixed Feelings

For four centuries Europeans had come to Africa as explorers, traders and missionaries. Now, with partition, the Europeans came as rulers. Their reception by their new subjects, the Africans, varied greatly. 'The Europeans have come to mend the country and put everything straight. God has sent them,' said one awe-struck man in the Congo in the early days. But an African chief at Mswata, near Stanleypool, was shrewder. He thought Europeans were only 'cows worth keeping, to be milked at pleasure'. He was willing to welcome these foreigners, for they brought things like cloth, tools and medicine!

Whether or not an African was openly hostile to Europeans depended very much on where he lived. In southern Africa thousands lost land they had previously cultivated: but north of the Zambezi the total number of people who suffered by European settlement was small.

There were plenty of individuals and peoples who gained from colonial rule. The Germans in East Africa (Tanganyika) trained many Swahili as soldiers, policemen and government clerks, with the result that they became a privileged class amongst other Africans. In Uganda, the Baganda people who joined British colonial regiments received great rewards in social developments of all kinds: roads, schools, hospitals were built by the British for them. Peoples such as these decided that resistance to Europeans was simply not worth it. They thought they could gain more by negotiating and bargaining. Of those who challenged a colonial power, news spread of their fate. The British, French and Belgians deposed the tribal rulers and confiscated land. 'The Maxim Gun commands respect,' said one African.

Grievances

By the 1920s the real meaning of colonial rule seemed clear to many Africans: exploitation. To the British, French and Belgians it meant slowly but efficiently developing the resources of

54

an area. To a number of Africans it meant being used for selfish purposes, as in the Congo.

Real grievances soon built up. African ideas on land and work were so completely different from the European that resentment was inevitable. When the British began dividing the land in Kenya into 'parcels' called Crown Land or Native Reserves, they came into conflict with a vital African principle. By long tradition land which was unoccupied could not be owned; land was like air and water—it should be freely available. However, the French in their colonies declared they owned the land by right of conquest, and in 1904 all vacant land was made state property. But what was 'vacant' land? The shifting cultivation of some African peoples made some land only appear vacant for a few years. The British government made a similar declaration in the Gold Coast, but a storm of protest arose, supported by the missionary newspapers, who called it 'civilized robbery and British brigandism'.

Taxes were another grievance, and they were closely linked with attitudes to work. As we have seen, the Europeans wished to make each colony self-supporting. So the population was taxed. In areas like Kenya and Rhodesia this served the useful purpose (to the Europeans) of making the Africans seek labouring jobs on the white farms; for this they were paid in cash, which they could then use to pay their taxes. In other places colonial governments themselves wanted labour for jobs like road-building or porterage. Work of this nature was demanded instead of a cash tax, but many Africans objected that this was almost forced labour. Why, they said, should able-bodied men be compelled to do jobs that used to be thought fit only for women or slaves!

To most Africans the idea of working to a timetable was quite new. Also, working regularly in order to earn money to buy personal things was very different from the village way of life where most things were shared. Hence Africans worked for Europeans for as short a time as possible especially as the low wages meant they could not eat as well as if they farmed. European officials and settlers could not understand such an attitude of mind and put it down to idleness. The idea grew up that Africans would not work unless they were forced to. Under French colonial laws every man between eighteen and sixty years had to work for a certain number of days for the state. This compulsion was one of the most hated features of French colonialism. And working conditions were often bad: poor housing and little food. In the German Cameroons too, men from the malaria-free highlands found they had to work in the mosquito-infested plantations near the coast; only 10 per cent ever saw their homes again.

Racial Discrimination

There is a fable told in the Cameroons which says: 'God went walking together with His three sons—a white man, a black man and a gorilla. The last two lost their way, and God went on walking with the white man only.' We saw in chapter 1 that the Europeans and Africans treated each other on roughly equal terms in the sixteenth and seventeenth centuries. By the nineteenth century European industrial supremacy quite easily became a racial superiority.

Those Africans who were benefiting from missionary education were especially bitter about this. They resented views expressed by men like the explorer, Stanley, 'It is good for the African to be drilled and disciplined and made to work'; and by the Belgian lawyer, Edmund Picard, who wrote in 1896: 'In spite of all our humanitarian goodwill we have to acknowledge the irreducible difference of race. Like monkeys, the blacks are good imitators. White scorns black, and black shows a natural submission, a childish humility.'

One result of the speed of the partition of Africa was that Europeans were controlling the destinies of millions of people they did not understand. Europeans could with some justice declare that 'Africans are backward'. But two false conclusions were drawn from this: that Africans were almost all equally backward; and that they were permanently backward.

Educated Africans today, like Kofi Busia, think this was the most serious failure of colonial rule. It was, he says, 'a failure in human relations—things came first, not human beings'. Europeans tended to see Africans as a mass of units—as 'hut-taxpayers' or as 'native labour', rarely as individuals. This attitude was not such a problem in the early days of colonial rule. At this time the few white men mixed with, and often lived quite close to Africans. Later officials and settlers increased in number, and they brought their families with them. African and European family life drew apart and a colour-bar soon developed. European social activities and clubs were barred to non-whites. A European wife, whose knowledge of the African was through inexperienced servants only, often decided *all* Africans were like this, and refused to mix with people she regarded as inferior.

Gradually a bitterness crept into European-African relations. A Senegalese poet, David Diop, who looks back at colonial days with anger, has written:

> The white man has killed my father;
> The white man, his hands red with black blood,
> With lordly voice, turned to me:
> 'Hey boy, a drink, a napkin, water.'

Perhaps the whole racial question in colonial Africa is summed up by a Congolese teacher, who said: 'If only they had treated us as human beings.' But for many Europeans in Africa Kipling summed up *their* attitude:

> But he does not talk my talk,
> I cannot feel his mind;
> I see the face, and the eyes and the mouth,
> But not the soul behind.

1939–45: The Watershed of Colonial Rule

There was, then, a feeling of discontent among some Africans. Ndabaningi Sithole, a Rhodesian African, wrote, 'we were in the early days simply overawed and perplexed. The white man's house that moves on water, his bird that is not like other birds, his monster that spits fire and smoke amazed us.' In time ordinary Africans reacted to their colonial masters in different ways. Many clearly resented a European-imposed colour-bar, but were happy to earn money to raise their standard of living, or to learn the techniques of the modern world. Others showed more obvious hostility. In Nigeria alone six areas of riot and rebellion occurred between 1906 and 1929, and 200 African leaders were in exile in the 1920s. Despite this in 1939 each European nation thought colonial rule was firmly rooted in Africa.

But the period 1939–45 proved to be its watershed. The War

Ronald Searle's famous *Punch* cartoon on the stirring of African nationalism

destroyed much of the prestige of the white man. Sithole noted:
'After spending four years hunting white enemy soldiers, the
African will never again regard them as gods.' African soldiers
on active service were better fed, clothed and paid than at home,
and many of them learned to read. When they returned home
in 1945 they were very dissatisfied with the conditions there.

Besides the personal experiences of the soldiers, Africans heard of the Atlantic Charter—the document of freedom signed by Churchill and Roosevelt during the war. It said they would, 'respect the right of all peoples to choose the form of government under which they will live'. The fact that British and French statesmen declared later that this did not include colonial peoples made little difference, for the idea had caught on. Finally, strong as colonial power looked, there was one great flaw: education.

African Nationalist Leaders

The mission schools had provided a valuable supply of clerks and junior officials for the colonial governments in the early days. In time each power developed its own ideas. When a few Africans in French and Portuguese colonies showed educational promise, they would be brought to study in Paris or Lisbon. Here they became an élite or privileged class, more European in outlook than African. A Senegalese leader said, 'We were Frenchmen in dark skins.' The Belgians felt there was no place for an élite in the Congo, and so concentrated on a technical education to turn some Africans into skilled workers for the copper mines of Katanga.

The British had rather a muddled policy. They allowed the church mission schools to improve their educational standards, and long before 1940 a number of educated Africans were leaving them to look for well-paid jobs with opportunities. They found them difficult to obtain. In places, under Lord Lugard's system, the only important positions of wealth and power were shared between the traditional African chiefs and British officials. There seemed no place here for a western-educated élite. Lugard himself was nasty to such Africans, referring to them as 'trousered blacks'.

This then was the flaw. The British educated people, and then refused them an opportunity to get on. The French gave them opportunity, but only in France itself—not in their home-land, Africa. These men were Africa's early nationalists, men who wanted freedom from foreign control. For most there was no question of going back to the old, tribal way of life. They accepted the modern world, but they wanted to run it themselves.

59

9 Nasser and the Egyptian Revolution

Nasser Plans a Revolution

'Where is dignity? Where is nationalism? It has all disappeared, and the nation lies asleep like the inhabitants of a cave. Who can wake them up, those miserable creatures?'

A young Egyptian, only seventeen years old and full of despair, wrote this in 1935. His name was Gamal Abdul Nasser. Already he had a scar on his forehead, from a police revolver bullet which had grazed him during a student demonstration in Cairo. Like several other young Egyptians he detested the weak government of Egypt, the almost total power of the big landowners and, particularly, the presence of British troops. Since 1922 Egypt was supposed to have been an independent country, but Britain still controlled his country's foreign policy and the rich Suez Canal zone.

For 2,500 years Egypt had been ruled by various foreigners: Persians, Greeks, Romans, Arabs and Turks. The British were the latest. During the Second World War Nasser, now an army officer, and many Egyptians were appalled when the country they loved was fought across by British and German/Italian armies; 1942 was the turning point in Nasser's early life. Just before the battle at El Alamein, the British ambassador in Cairo wanted to make sure that the Egyptian government and especially King Farouk were not plotting with the Germans. The royal palace was surrounded by British tanks and a British 'suggestion' for prime minister forced on the king. Patriotic feeling rose against Great Britain, and sheer hatred replaced resentment of her presence in Egypt. 'As for the Army,' Nasser wrote, 'the episode had a new, electrifying effect on our spirits.'

A few officers met secretly in a Cairo suburb, and a revolution was born. They called themselves the 'Free Officers' and began planning two events. The first was the destruction of the pashas —the old, greedy landowning class ('pasha' roughly means a lord). To do this properly King Farouk would also have to go. Second, Egypt must be rid of British power.

Captain Nasser was the patient leader of the Free Officers. The group was difficult to control, and in its early years haphazard in its planning. By the end of the war, however, he had developed a disciplined organization. One of the other officers, Anwar Sadat, has given us details of this. A central committee controlled quite separate sections like one on finance, one on recruiting, one on security and one on terrorism. A special feature was the small cell: a few soldiers or students who only met and planned amongst themselves. Thus Nasser was able to control a wide and growing organization without many members knowing who the other members were.

Nasser had particular difficulty with the terrorist group. For instance, Sadar himself wanted at one time to blow up the British Embassy, but Nasser refused, on the grounds that it was a senseless act which would not persuade the British to leave. Nasser's aim was revolution, not just a small-scale revolt, and he was, says one writer, 'not a man to be led away by dreams'.

He was a tall, impressive man. People who met him noticed his remarkable eyes and large-ish nose. He always lived quietly and was a devout Muslim. In public he was a reserved figure, but in private he could be very emotional. One man who knew him described him as 'a man of ice—and fire'.

The First Enemy: the Pashas and Farouk

The wealth of Egypt was concentrated in very few hands. In the 1940s the population was 19 million. Most were without land, and of the $2\frac{1}{2}$ million landowners, nearly 2 million owned under one acre each. The Egyptian peasants or 'fellahin' have been described as 'the most downtrodden people in the world, living out their miserable, short lives in slime and squalor.' The pashas, the landed nobility of Egypt, were descended from the Turks. They showed off their wealth to the world in the most dazzling fashion, and used it to gain control of the main political party, the Wafd. At the head of this ruling class was 'the richest, grossest and greediest of them all—King Farouk'.

Farouk used to be a respected monarch, slim, handsome and a serious young man. But by the late 1940s he had become grotesquely fat, and he spent his personal riches (his income was £2 million a year) in such a silly way that he became a buffoon in the eyes of his people and the world. He spent so long gam-

61

bling in Monte Carlo that he had little time for state business.

Thus Farouk was not only loathed by his subjects; he was unable to rule efficiently either. This was shown in 1948. In this year part of Palestine was given by the United Nations to form the Jewish state of Israel. Arabs in the Middle East and North Africa resented this, and Egypt launched an attack on the new state. Farouk's Royal Army was a miserable failure. Nasser, now a major, fought well in a small part of the war front, but bravery was useless in this contest. Food for the troops failed to arrive; guns were old; bullets were either in short supply or did not fit the weapons. News of a great scandal raced through Cairo's streets. Men out for a quick profit had been supplying faulty arms and dud ammunition. In the view of junior officers like Nasser, the efforts of the Army High Command were hopeless and there were several examples of cowardice.

By 1949 Farouk had lost the loyalty of the Army. From this point he was a doomed man.

The Night of 22 July 1952

Nasser was now quite sure *what* to do. He wrote, 'The Middle East is searching for a hero', and he clearly saw himself in the role. Yet for a year or so he was unsure *how* to act. His Free Officers Movement toyed with the idea of blocking the Suez Canal, as anti-British feeling was strong in the country. Also there seemed a chance of cooperating with another revolutionary group in Egypt, the Muslim Brotherhood, who believed that only terrorism and faith in Mahomet could save Egypt. But by 1952 Nasser was convinced that the Officers must themselves strike at the heart of the problem: Farouk and his government.

Nasser remained cautious. He planned action for 'sometime in 1954'. A senior officer, General Neguib, had been converted to Nasser's ideas, and he was expected to give the Movement some respectability abroad when it acted.

Farouk was not foolish enough to be unaware that something was going on. He quietly arranged for much of his enormous personal fortune to be banked in Switzerland. He also tried to split the officers. He had no idea who the conspirators were, so he lashed out with army postings to distant parts. Neguib was on this list. The Free Officers met on 10 July 1952 to consider the situation, and one of them wrote later:

'Gamal and a friend came to my house, and asked me to play Rimsky-Korsakov's *Scheherazade*. Gamal listened attentively with dreamy eyes. At the last note, he stood up, lifted the needle off the record and said, abruptly, "We shall strike at the beginning of next month."'

Within ten days Nasser faced a new problem. He heard that fourteen Free Officers were about to be arrested. So action was brought forward to the evening of 22 July. Army Headquarters were to be seized and all key communication points in Cairo were to be occupied. Drama increased when Nasser heard during the afternoon of the 22nd that a few senior officers were planning a move of their own: the arrest of Nasser. However, the Army High Command must have thought there was no immediate danger and Nasser of minor importance for they only sent a captain. Anyway he was a poor choice for he joined the Free Officers, and Nasser moved. Army HQ was taken. At midnight radio and police stations in Cairo were occupied. By one o'clock in the morning the city was in Free Officer hands, and Farouk, holidaying in Alexandria, was given three days to get out of the country.

One of the important revolutions of modern times had taken place. Its list of casualties: two men dead; seven wounded. No persecution of men who had supported Farouk took place. For this moderation Nasser gained prestige in the eyes of the world, which had been expecting a bloodthirsty revenge.

Quickly, Nasser showed faith with the Egyptian people. In September 1952 the great landed estates were broken up, and a law decreed that no one could own more than 200 acres. The rest was given to poor fellahin in small plots. Also he set in motion a programme of industrialization. But food for the people and power for his industries was an immediate need. He already had in mind a scheme for this: a huge dam across the River Nile. Within four years, however, this scheme became entangled in Anglo-American relations.

The Second Enemy: Britain

Nasser hoped he could get rid of British influence in Egypt by negotiation. For a time things went well. The two countries

Nasser's problem: relations with the communist powers and the Western world

agreed to leave the Sudan which they had been ruling in suspicious partnership since 1899. Soon after this Nasser scored a great triumph, and a treaty was signed whereby Britain was to evacuate her troops from the Suez Canal by 1956. To some people in Britain this was a retreat, for, as we have seen, concern for the security of the route to India and the East had drawn Britain into Egypt back in 1882. Yet her statesmen fully appreciated how air power and the atomic bomb had made nonsense of the idea of keeping the Canal against Egyptian opposition.

Then things went wrong. The United States, fearful of Russia's growing influence in the Middle East, tried to persuade Egypt to join a defence pact. But Nasser did not want any further entanglements with foreign powers for his country. This idea was strengthened when in 1955 he met the Indian leader, Pandit Nehru, and came under his influence. The two men thought Africa and Asia would best be served if they kept aloof from the Cold War between Communist and Western powers.

So, whilst negotiating a huge and vital loan from the United States and Britain for building the Aswan Dam, Nasser was also willing to buy arms from the communists. This led to a crisis in Western relations with Egypt. These had already been strained when at an earlier meeting Eden the British premier, treated Nasser, so he complained later, 'like a junior official who could not be expected to understand international politics'. At this point the United States and Britain clearly thought the evacuation of British troops from the Canal Zone would be the signal for Soviet Russian power to move in. So they withdrew their offer of 70 million dollars for the Dam in an attempt to make Nasser think again.

Nasser refused to be bullied or blackmailed, and he took immediate action. On 20 July 1956 he nationalized the Suez Canal, and announced that the Dam would be built with the profits. Britain prepared for war, and in October, with French and Israeli forces, invaded Egypt. They hoped to bring Nasser to heel with a quick victory. It was a tragic miscalculation.

Pressure from the United Nations was enormous, and in view of such criticism Britain and France withdrew, without a military victory. For them the expedition had been a total disaster. Nasser seized all British property in Cairo and the Canal Zone. The Suez crisis for Nasser solved the problem of his second enemy. At last Egypt was fully independent. The lesson for the rest of Africa was obvious.

10 Kwame Nkrumah of Ghana

The Cocoa Riots of 1948

'Peoples of the colonies must have the right to elect their own governments. Colonial and subject peoples of the world, unite!' These words were used at a meeting in Manchester in 1945. Whilst Britain and Europe celebrated victory at the end of the Second World War, a group of Africans were meeting to plan another victory: the end of European rule in Africa. The war had had a powerful effect. Its purpose they said, had been to fight for the right to freedom. The United Nations with its new visions was there to prove it.

Then ex-servicemen who had fought for the Allies returned to Africa. They had been strongly influenced by Asian nationalists; also a few thought there was a lesson for Africans in the defeat of European colonial powers like Germany, Italy and Vichy France. In the Gold Coast they came back to a troubled scene. Cocoa was the country's main crop and export, but a swollen shoot disease had been affecting production. The only way to stamp it out was total destruction of any trees with the disease. British colonial officials began the process, long and difficult because millions of trees were showing signs of it. Discontent grew amongst the Gold Coast farmers who made their living from the cocoa crop.

Market traders, too, found their livelihood threatened, when early in 1948 the big British and French export and import combines introduced the 'conditional sale' system into West Africa. These combines dealt with many different kinds of goods, some of which proved slow sellers from their warehouses. So they insisted that if a small trader came to buy a quantity of a popular product he had to accept a less popular one as well. For instance, if six yards of cloth was bought then six enamel plates had also to be taken and paid for. Immediately profits in the local West African markets dropped sharply.

In the Gold Coast traders allied with the cocoa farmers to protest. Disappointed ex-servicemen joined them. In Accra

66

rioting broke out: twenty-nine people were killed and £2 million worth of property damaged. A British official wrote: 'On 27 February 1948 the Gold Coast was a model colony. On the 1 March it was a shambles.' Some leading agitators were detained by the police for a while; one was Kwame Nkrumah, who had been at the Manchester meeting three years earlier.

'That Scallawag, Nkrumah'

The British government took the Accra rioting very seriously. An investigation under Sir Henry Coussey revealed much dissatisfaction. The British then said they were quite willing to allow some of the more respectable Africans to have a voice in the colony's government—men like the chiefs, lawyers and the richer cocoa farmers. These men had in fact already formed a small political party, and Coussey asked them for their ideas.

Out of their discussions came a new constitution for the Gold Coast, which is one of the great landmarks in modern African history. It was the first of the many steps which decolonized the continent. The Gold Coast was to have an African parliament and a government of eight Africans and three Europeans. The British government would be represented by a governor.

Into this situation burst Kwame Nkrumah, and African politics has never been the same since. He denounced the Coussey constitution as an 'imperialist fraud' and formed his own political party, the CPP or Convention Peoples' Party. Its slogan was 'Self-government Now'. He shouted for strikes and a boycott of British goods by his supporters among the poorer farmers and masses of the coastal towns.

Nkrumah had a magnetic personality and great organizing genius. He toured the country collecting support and funds for his party. This was too much for the British colonial government. 'That scallawag, Nkrumah', as a British official called him, was arrested and sent to prison for three years. But he was already a national hero and the people looked up to him as a modern Moses. Word got around that no gaol could hold him, and that he used to slip out at night disguised as a white cat. His party gained a sweeping victory in the 1951 elections. The efficiency of the CPP and the obvious influence of the imprisoned Nkrumah was so impressive that he was released. He immediately became prime minister!

67

Show Boy and Osagyefo

Nkrumah was now well up the ladder of power. As he said himself, 'Seek ye first the political kingdom and all things will be added unto you.' Six years later Britain felt the Gold Coast was rich enough and stable enough to give it independence. In those years Nkrumah owed his continued authority to two things. There was the trust and goodwill that developed between himself and the British Governor, Sir Charles Arden-Clarke. The Governor was a remarkable man, one of the few 'colonialists' who worked sincerely to bring an end to imperial rule—on condition that the colony was able to look after itself.

Also Nkrumah was a master of the political arena. He was fully aware that there was much opposition to himself and his party from the Ashanti chiefs to the north. They resented the upstart Nkrumah who had edged them from the position of power which was traditionally theirs. CPP strength came from the young men and women of the more southerly cocoa growing and trading areas. Many were immigrants from the northern country areas, where tribal chiefs were still wealthy and powerful, exercising considerable local control, according to Lugard's indirect rule idea. In the eyes of many Africans the chiefs were just pawns of British colonialism. They were also envied for the high incomes from mining and timber works on their land. In central areas of the Gold Coast, like Kumasi, where loyalties to the chiefs or the CPP were blurred, violence between rival supporters, in the form of house-burning and political murder, was common.

Nkrumah made good use of these feelings. He called the chiefs 'black squires' and accused them of being half-hearted in the Gold Coast independence movement. He also used his personality to the full in campaigning for political support. Market women in Accra would shout 'Show Boy' whenever he toured the place. The name stuck and the power of the Nkrumah legend grew.

In 1951 the CPP had shown itself capable and well supported. But before granting independence the British insisted that another election be held. It was savagely fought, but Nkrumah's party machine triumphed and the CPP won 72 out of 104 seats in parliament.

Independence Day was early in 1957. Nkrumah was later

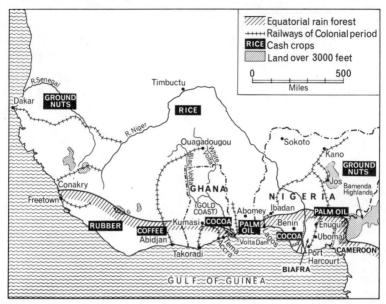

hailed as 'Osagyefo', the Great Redeemer, and the British colony of the Gold Coast became the sovereign African country of Ghana (the name came from the powerful medieval state in·West Africa). Ghana was well prepared for independence. Her cocoa exports, now recovered from the setbacks of the late 1940s, meant considerable prosperity for the people as well as cash reserves for the government. If Nkrumah could bind the different groups in Ghana—the chiefs, the merchants, the lawyers, the masses—into a nation he would set an example for the rest of Africa. But the less developed north and the Ashanti of the centre were still highly suspicious of 'Osagyefo'.

The Fallen Idol

Nkrumah wanted three things: total political power, a rich state and leadership of a united Africa. They were wild dreams and events proved that the first contradicted the other two.

He tackled with energy the many problems in turning a tribal, rural society into an advanced, modern state. He was a socialist and regarded his first duty to be that of raising the ordinary people's standard of living. Schools were built, miles of roads laid, the telegraph system extended and the number of hospital

69

Women gaily dressed for Ghana's independence celebrations, 6 March 1957. A Nkrumah portrait is on the dress on the left

beds increased. All these cost money, and his £200 million credit at independence soon disappeared. And Nkrumah never really understood the accusation that other expensive schemes were only projects for his own prestige. The magnificent £3 million Accra–Tema motorway had few vehicles on it, and a great State House for ceremonial functions which cost £6 million is little used even today.

His most famous project was the Volta River Hydroelectric Scheme. It was costly (£150 million) yet impressive and would be of enormous value to Ghana's future prosperity. As part of the scheme a big artificial harbour was to be built at Tema. Nkrumah planned all this as the beginning of Ghana's industrial revolution. By the mid-1960s the main dam, 2,200 feet wide and 240 feet high, was complete, and a lake behind it, 250 miles long, began to take shape. Yet the massive cost and the dependence on American investors' money provoked criticism. Nkrumah, it was argued, had his priorities wrong:

Ghana was not rich enough for such an undertaking. Taxation rose, and so did the cost of living—30 per cent in the two years 1964 and 1965.

Ghana was too small a stage for Nkrumah. He liked to see newspaper references to himself as 'Nkrumah of Africa'. However, his support for a unified Black Africa was looked on with mistrust by other African leaders like Nasser, Nyerere and Kenyatta. At home, too, his diplomatic contacts with the Soviet Union and Communist China were viewed as dangerous.

Prosperity at home and prestige abroad needed a stable government in Ghana. For Nkrumah stability meant unquestioned power, and he sought this ruthlessly. His 'personality' was everywhere: on postage stamps, coins, in neon lights, bronze statues and street names. His original energy and political genius slowly ebbed away; he became vain and fearful of rivals. He abolished all opposition parties, and Ghana became a One-Party State. Nkrumah now had complete control and could dismiss army generals and ministers—and even judges who in a democracy should be free from government interference.

Nkrumah thought a One-Party State imperative. The people, the party and the state were, to him, all one, and it was his answer to the problem of making a nation out of the old tribal groupings. To others the way he went about this discredited him. Kofi Busia, one of his leading opponents, said; 'Single party power was seized, not granted by the voters.' In 1964, 93 per cent of Ghanaians were supposed to have voted 'Yes' to the idea, but foreign journalists saw all kinds of peculiar practices. One reported: 'There was a mixture of intimidation and ballot-rigging which ranged from farcical to brutal.' In some polling booths the 'No' boxes were sealed with tape!

The Preventive Detention Act of 1958 had given Nkrumah wide powers. A man could be detained in prison for five years without appearing in court, if he acted 'in a manner prejudicial to the security of the State'. Within a few years even Nkrumah's close advisers feared for their own safety. One of them remarked: 'Anybody can go and cause the detention of anybody.' Yet, secretly, opposition to Nkrumah grew. Those who were disgusted with his vanity and policies joined forces with those who knew that merely expressing an opinion was dangerous.

4

The end came suddenly and bloodlessly. Nkrumah, on a visit to China in February 1966, heard that he had been deposed. A group of army officers seized power; they had been appalled at Nkrumah's personal extravagance in a country where, said one, 'it was shameful to see a Ghanaian soldier in tattered and ragged uniforms'. Over the radio came details of Nkrumah's misuse of power, and the market women of Accra stamped underfoot their pictures of the man they had once hailed as 'Show Boy'. A leader of the army revolt wrote later: 'Nkrumah could have been a great man. He became the symbol of emergent Africa. But he developed a strange taste for absolute power.' Nkrumah went into exile, where he remains.

Ghana used to be a prosperous, advanced state, the envy of many of her less well-off neighbours. But today she is the envy of no one. The Army Council has set about reconstructing her economy, and many of Nkrumah's prestige projects have been cut down. Politicians, now free from his repressive police system, are working out a new constitution. But it will be many years before Ghana once more claims to set an example for Africa.

11 Conflict and Terror in Algeria

Angry Feelings from the Start

Europeans came to Algeria in 1830. They were French and they were conquerors. For centuries Italian, Spanish and French traders in the Mediterranean had protested that Algeria's Barbary Coast harboured nests of pirates and ruthless seahawks. At the same time an Englishman voiced a different view: Algiers was 'a great place of trade and merchandise, with 3,000 merchant families and 2,000 shops'. There were big market towns which distributed the mutton and cereals produced in the fertile coastal plain between the Atlas Mountains and the sea. Much trade also went across the Sahara southwards.

So, when the French expedition claimed to be ridding the Mediterranean of the pirates it was only a half truth. This became even clearer in the years after 1830 when French settlers, called 'colons', came to Algeria. They did not want to grow crops just for a local market; they intended developing a rich export trade in wine. The 4,000 acres under vines in 1830 rose to three-quarters of a million by 1953. Yet grain production stayed roughly the same—to feed a population that had trebled. These figures spelt prosperity for the colon, and poverty for the mass of Berber and Arab peoples of Algeria.

From the start the French found warlike tribes on the Atlas and Saharan regions a menace to the valuable vineyards. And when a great 'jihad' or holy war was declared in 1832 by Abd al-Qadir against the French, small, brutal campaigns broke out and continued for half a century. These drew French armies more and more into the interior where Arab and Frenchman treated each other with ferocity. This shedding of blood was to recur many times in the next hundred years.

The Colon and the Algerian

By 1880 there were 350,000 colons. Many were poor Frenchmen whose vineyards in south France had been ruined by disease; others were Spaniards and Italians escaping from the

73

The Maghrib. North-west Africa showing the Algerian war

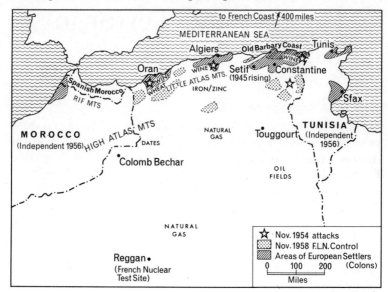

overcrowding in the cities of their homeland. A few were rich, like Henri Borgeaud who became Algeria's 'King of the Vine'. As a group they were arrogant and selfish. A French prime minister wrote of the colon in 1892, 'We have found him limited. It is hard to make him understand that other rights exist, besides his own, in an Arab country, and that the native is not a race to be enslaved at his whim.'

Half a century later the colon had not changed his views. He was full of scorn for the 'primitive Arab'. An article in the French newspaper, *L'Express* in 1955 said colons had 'the sincere conviction that they are born to be masters, as others are born to be slaves'.

The French government regarded Algeria as part of France, and thus the colons were citizens of France. They elected their own representatives to Paris, who used their influence to get considerable sums of money spent on Algerian development. Port facilities and communications were improved, and the roads of north-west Africa (the area is called the Maghrib) were some of the finest in the continent.

In theory the Algerians could become citizens on equal terms with the colons. They first had to give up their Muslim religion for Christianity, and secondly be literate. A few were

74

well-educated and spoke French better than Arabic, but even in 1950, 90 per cent of Algerians could neither read nor write. The rural areas were poor and many young men drifted to the towns in search of better opportunities. Half of all Algerian workers were employed for only a hundred days in a year; thousands of others were dependent on money being sent to them from relations who had gone to European France. Because of these very pronounced differences in education and employment, one Algerian, Ferhat Abbas, lamented that although he longed to see the French go, 'I would not die for an Algerian Fatherland, because no such Fatherland exists'.

Civil War and Terror

1945: the end of the Second World War. In it many Algerians had fought for France with honour. One young man, Ben Bella, received the Croix de Guerre. A 'new deal' for Algeria was expected. As the war in Europe drew to a close in May, parades were organized by Algerian nationalists. Some of these, like Abbas, had long demanded equal rights and opportunities for prosperity with the colons. Others wanted more: independence.

On 8 May in Setif a 'Victory over Germany' parade began. The local police became frightened and tried to seize the nationalist banners. The demonstrators resisted and shots were fired, resulting in the deaths of a hundred or so French officials and colons. The French took widespread and savage reprisals. Algerian villages along the coast were bombed from the air and shelled from the sea; at least 20,000 were killed, although some put the figure as high as 45,000.

Algerian nationalists, unable to gain their ends by peaceful means, now planned in secret. Ben Bella and other young men quarrelled with the older moderates like Abbas, and formed the National Liberation Front or FLN, to lead the revolt against French rule. Its organization was long and difficult, but on 1 November 1954 at 1 a.m. they acted. Thirty synchronized attacks were made on French military targets by 2,500 men armed with hunting rifles. The Algerian revolution had begun.

The FLN knew the struggle would take many years and that the 1 November had been only a call to arms. After this they split into small groups and withdrew to the Kabylia and Aures mountain region behind and to the east of Algiers. From here

75

they waged guerrilla warfare, with attacks by 'patriots' and 'rebels' on civilians and soldiers alike becoming a regular part of daily life. Within twelve months burning farms, smashed railways and a successful boycott of French tobacco created an atmosphere of insecurity in Algeria.

In 1956 the FLN struck at the capital and for four months the Battle of Algiers raged. By now the French had organized powerful forces against what they called 'primitive, bloodthirsty barbarians'. General Jacques Massu and his crack 10th Paratroop Division arrived from France. The Casbah, the old walled Arab quarter of the city was sealed off completely with barbed wire, as the French regarded this area as the centre of nationalist power. Within a year Massu's overwhelming force and his use of torture broke resistance in Algiers.

Bitterness had reached such proportions that many moderate colons felt they were defending a way of life which was now dead. At the same time a fanatical colon was heard seriously to suggest, 'If we Europeans each kill fourteen Algerians the problem will be solved.'

Enter de Gaulle 1958

In four years the FLN Algerian Army had grown from a few thousand badly armed 'rebels' to 125,000 well trained guerrillas, armed by other North African countries. But they faced 400,000 French, using helicopters and armed with the latest weapons. Slowly this force closed frontiers and broke up the FLN. Some leaders, amongst them Ben Bella, were captured and imprisoned in France; others fled to Tunisia or Egypt.

The Algerians were not pinning their hopes only on a military victory. They appealed for world sympathy towards their cause, and were rewarded when the Battle of Algiers received enormous publicity in the newspapers of the United States and Europe. The FLN also anticipated that public opinion in France itself would weary of a long and costly struggle. This proved correct, for the real turning point in the war came in Paris. The fighting in Algeria was costing the French tax-payer millions of francs, and no government seemed able to secure victory. Remembering the soldier-hero of the Second World

The Casbah in Algiers provided excellent hide-outs for FLN guerrilla fighters

War, the cry went up: 'de Gaulle to power'. He became premier, and a quick, successful solution to the Algerian question was confidently expected. He began by removing some of the extremist officers in the French Army, because he disliked the reputation for torture which the 'paras' had gained. This was not at all to the liking of the more fanatical colons and they sensed a betrayal.

De Gaulle was soon convinced that a military victory would not settle Algeria. In 1961 he proposed to start negotiating with the nationalists. Alarm spread through the colons and in the Algerian units of the French Army. Four generals determined to seize power. At seven o'clock in the morning of 22 April the Algiers radio broadcast, 'The Armed Forces have taken over.' They intended, they said, to 'keep Algeria French'. Paratroops were soon in control of all the key buildings and the French Air Forces at the Maison Blanche Airfield in Algiers prepared to fly other paras to France to take control of the government there. Panic words over Paris Radio on the 23rd said that an airborne descent on the capital 'might be imminent'.

But the planned seizure of power was a fiasco. A sandstorm swept Maison Blanche at the critical moment; some important generals refused their support; and rumours spread that there was not enough money in Algeria to pay the soldiers. By midnight on the 25th it was all over. Troops loyal to the Parisian Government quickly regained control in Algeria. Leading conspirators amongst the senior officials and colons went into hiding to form their own secret army, the OAS. It was strongly opposed to de Gaulle, moderate colons and particularly Algerian independence. In the next few years, whilst de Gaulle worked out a settlement with the FLN, the OAS caused havoc throughout Algeria. At one time they tried to fire the entire Casbah. These were desperate men, and with their ruthless 'plastic bomb' sabotage, they seemed determined to destroy the country they could no longer rule.

Ben Bella and Independence

De Gaulle agreed to Algerian independence in June 1962. Prominent nationalists were released from prison; Ben Bella was amongst them. As soon as the news was announced colons began leaving Algeria. In one day, 20 May, a round-the-clock airlift was necessary at Maison Blanche airfield. The exit of so many colons led to a crisis in the country. With them went much money and considerable technical skill. Jobs became scarce; soon two million were unemployed.

Ben Bella was hailed as the 'strong man' to deal with the problem. He ruled Algeria with determination for the next three years, offering hope for a better future to the ordinary Algerians. Food, schools for their children, medical help and cheap housing—all seemed possible with a peaceful, efficient government. On two key problems, famine and education, Ben Bella took a close personal interest.

A street in Algeria after a guerrilla bomb attack

In September 1962 he launched 'Operation Ploughing', with promises of tractors from abroad. But the Algerian peasants, the 'fellahin', just sat back and waited; they thought other people were coming to plough the fields for them! Ben Bella wrote that he had to go and explain to the village leaders that 'we had just got to roll up our shirtsleeves and start ploughing with anything available. I penalised incompetent administrators. I requisitioned seed and ploughs on the spot.'

Whilst investigating the other problem, education, Ben Bella noticed the shoe-shine boys, poor children who had come into the towns from the rural areas, but could find no other job. He was disgusted, he said, at 'the sight of swarms of thin and ragged children on their knees at the feet of healthy adults; they seemed to me symbolic of the humiliation of the "native"'. He wanted these and other Algerian children at school, saying 'arrogant and lazy people will have to do what I do: buy a brush and clean their own shoes'. Although he was criticized for showing Algeria's weakness, he appealed to France for volunteers to come and teach. They came.

Ben Bella represents Algeria at the United Nations Assembly

But cries of 'dictator' grew louder during Ben Bella's rule. Ex-FLN fighters distrusted him, for he had spent the 'revolution' years in a French gaol; others thought he was playing traitor by allowing France to keep oil rights in the Sahara. In June 1965 his enemies triumphed. A few shots rang out during the night at Ben Bella's home. No one has seen him since, although it is thought he is imprisoned somewhere.

A more cautious, if less colourful, man now rules Algeria. Colonel Boumedienne keeps firm control with Africa's third strongest army (after South Africa and Egypt). Yet he is still no nearer solving the same problems Ben Bella faced: unemployment, reliance on American food aid, and how to use the iron and natural gas supplies in the Sahara for Algeria's benefit.

12 Land Hunger in Kenya

An Iron Snake

In the 1890s a survey was made for a railway to link the new British colonial area around Lake Victoria with the East African ports. The difficulties and dangers were considerable. Running from Mombasa inland, the railway had to climb 7,000 feet, drop in a zigzag fashion along the sides of the Great Rift Valley, cross the Valley floor with its volcanoes and boiling mud areas, up again to 9,000 feet, and finally drop to the shores of the Lake. By 1903 it was finished. This railway, the 'iron snake' as the local Africans called it, brought the modern world, with its hope of prosperity to Kenya. It also brought problems, which had not been finally soived at Kenya's independence celebrations in 1963.

The cost of the Uganda Railway construction had been high. So the British government encouraged white men (British and South Africans) to buy land along the middle section of the route, where the soil was suitable for farming and the higher land cool enough for settlement. An early settler was Lord Delamere, a vigorous man, full of ideas. He introduced new farming methods, and by the 1920s a successful experiment with coffee provided a valuable crop for sale abroad. The settlers found their interests well looked after by the British Commissioner, Sir Charles Eliot. These two men, Delamere and Eliot, wanted to build the Highlands of East Africa into a white man's country, and according to European standards of the time, this was an ambitious and honourable idea. Rolling wheatfields and huge coffee and flax plantations soon appeared in limited areas.

The building of the Railway brought Indians to Kenya. They were easily controlled workers, 'more docile than local natives', said the employers. After the Uganda Railway was finished many stayed on to work as tradesmen in Mombasa or Nairobi. Some white settlers became worried as the Indians began dominating the commerce of the two towns. By 1920 there were

9,600 white settlers and officials, and 22,800 Indians in Kenya.
There were many hundreds of thousands of black men, too.

A visitor to Kenya wrote: 'There is in Nairobi keen political
and racial discord, all the materials for hot debate. The white
man versus black; Indian versus both. Behind—very close
behind—lie the appeals to force, by mobs or empires to decide

in a brutal fashion which of the sets of interests shall prevail.' The author of this interesting forecast of part of Kenya's future, made in 1908, was Winston Churchill.

In 1922 the British government said it was going to grant the political vote in Kenya to all British subjects, on condition that they had a certain level of education. Although this would only involve about 10 per cent of the Indians, they would numerically be a power to be reckoned with. Indo-European hostility flared up. A Kenya-Indian leader proclaimed his support for 'the annexation of this African territory to the Indian Empire'. The white settlers prepared a revolt: the Governor was to be kidnapped and held hostage until the British government gave up such pro-Indian acts. The rebellion never took place, because the London government retreated before powerful settler pressure. It contented itself with a declaration that 'Kenya was an African country in which the interests of the African were to be paramount.'

Ten years later the government in London marked off 17,000 square miles of the White Highlands, in which 'no other person than a European shall be entitled to acquire agricultural land'. It looked as if Lord Delamere's dream had come true. Africans, however, wondered about British sincerity on the subject of 'paramount African interests'.

The Kikuyu Nation

There is a Swahili song, popular in Kenya today, that has the lines:

> What is misery?
> It's a man without land.

It shows the strong feelings which land ownership has created in Kenya over the past half century. European settlers, supported by laws passed in London, took land away from the African tribes. In 1912 a treaty with the Masai had moved these semi-nomadic cattle herders from areas suitable for white settlement. But they still had plenty left.

Not so the Kikuyu. These peoples were farmers who tilled the land around the slopes of Mt Kenya. They shifted their cultivation gradually as the goodness in the thin soil was exhausted. During the nineteenth century the Kikuyu population grew

A Kikuyu elder. Men like this made up a council which governed the Kikuyu people

rapidly, and they spread outwards, but a sudden smallpox epidemic slowed this expansion down. As they recovered they found the Europeans had set a limit to the 'Kikuyu Reserve'. Resentment was widespread, for the Kikuyu were a prosperous, energetic community. They had no chiefs or kings, but governed themselves through village councils, rather like a loose clan system. Young men found the 'Reserves' offered few outlets for their ambitions. They could labour daily or weekly on the white farms, but discovered the settlers only paid them a low wage. This was enough, some Europeans argued, for the man himself —his family, who stayed in the Reserve could look after itself. Soon a 'squatter' system developed. A man brought his family to live in one hut on his employer's land. The low wage

84

remained, as his small plot of land was regarded as part of the pay. Young men could, of course, move to Nairobi or Mombasa, to work as clerks or labourers.

In these towns Kikuyu discontent was more obvious and could be used by a leader with a flair for organization. As with the Europeans and Indians, 1922 was a critical year for the Kikuyu. Two things brought matters to a head. First, the 'kipande' was introduced. This was an identity card with a thumb print, which all Africans over the age of sixteen had to carry; in it their work record was detailed. Secondly, all settlers agreed to reduce African labourers' wages from 10s. to 7s. a month: it was an appalling prospect for any Kikuyu with a large family.

So Harry Thuku, a Kikuyu clerk in Nairobi formed the Young Kikuyu Association to protest against such discrimination. At public meetings, attended by many thousands, he spoke vehemently, yet he could get little support from the reserves. Thuku was arrested as an agitator and a threat to public order in March 1922, and after a riot outside the prison where he was held, he was banished to a village in the distant Northern Frontier region of Kenya.

The white settlers thought that this was the end of 'the African Question'. For them, the Indians, growing rapidly in numbers and wealth, seemed more important. Settlers warned each other of 'the tentacles of this evil menace'.

Nevertheless, Harry Thuku had stirred Kikuyu nationalism. What had previously been a loose collection of peoples began to feel common bonds. The Kikuyu were on the way to becoming a nation. Thuku's Association had other able leaders to take over from him. One of them was Jomo Kenyatta.

Kenyatta, the 'Burning Spear'

For forty years this man was the symbol of first Kikuyu, then Kenyan, and in some ways African nationalism. He took over Kikuyu leadership in 1928, and made land ownership the central point in his campaign against British rule. He was then in his mid-thirties. He spoke out in Kenya with his Association's newspaper, and came to London in 1930 to put his case to the British government, but in vain. He travelled widely: back to Kenya, then to Moscow and a return to London to the University where he studied anthropology. He remained in Britain throughout the Second World War.

The decisive year was 1946. Kenyatta went back to Kenya to become later President of the newly formed political group, the Kenya African Union. Industry had grown considerably in Africa during the Second World War, and in Kenya the number of factory workers had risen to 10,000. Many of these lived in Nairobi, where wages were low and there was much tension. These workers turned to the KAU for a lead. Kenyatta's personality and oratory were compelling attractions. Tens of thousands came to listen to this big man with his grey-black beard, huge red ring and fly-whisk. By 1950 he had united most Kenya Africans in protest against British domination. One man wrote of 'Mzee', the Grand Old Man, as Kenyatta was known:

'The living, throbbing, hustling, laughing, crying, bursting mass of our people love him more than anything else they know. He is our chosen leader, and he alone will lead us out of the past, out of the deep pits of dark memories to the bright future of our country.'

Appeals were made by the European settlers to the government to exile this dangerous man, Kenyatta, and to crush African nationalism.

Mau Mau

With the memories of the treatment of Harry Thuku still in their minds, some of the Kikuyu turned to terrorism. The words 'Mau Mau' were heard for the first time. No one knows exactly where the phrase came from; the best explanation seems to be that it was a slightly altered form of the Kikuyu word for 'quit'. Police informers heard of the revival of old witchcraft practices and of secret oath-taking ceremonies, with weird, horrible, magical actions using sheep's eyes, banana leaves, goats and dead cats. Oaths were taken to kill Europeans and any Africans working for the colonial government. Atrocious murders occurred, in which the victims were literally chopped to pieces with a long, heavy knife, the panga.

On 20 October 1953 the British declared a state of emergency. Kenyatta and 183 other leading Africans were arrested. At his trial in a remote village Kenyatta was declared by the prosecution to be 'the master-mind' behind Mau Mau, and he

A young Mau Mau terrorist captured by security forces in Kenya

was imprisoned. There was a great deal of protest at this dubious justice: many thought the trial unfair and that only selected witnesses were allowed. Mau Mau continued to flourish, and in 1954 several battles were fought in the mountain forests of the Aberdare Range in the Kenyan Highlands. British army units adopted guerrilla tactics in an effort to end the protracted military struggle. By late 1956 only a few Kikuyu groups were left fighting in the remoter parts. At the same time 100,000 Kikuyu 'sympathizers' in the White Highlands and in the towns were rounded up and detained in large camps. This broke the back of Mau Mau and by 1960 the emergency was officially declared over.

The British treated Mau Mau as a highly organized piece of nastiness. Although the full story of these years has still to be written, it is thought today that Mau Mau was not a planned campaign. A properly organized rising could have killed most European settlers and officials in a few days. In fact very few Europeans were murdered. It was in fact a divided movement. Some members were small-time thugs paying off old scores against Africans; the terrible Lari Massacre of 1953, when several African villages were sacked and burned, was an example of this. Others were the 'freedom fighters of the forest'— genuine Mau Mau soldiers at war in their people's cause.

It is doubtful if Kenyatta could have 'master-minded' such a movement from prison. He was more of a martyr for the Kenya African's troubles. Yet even after seven years in prison the Governor of Kenya called him 'the African leader to darkness and death', and refused to release him. The British colonial government seemed unwilling to accept the argument that Mau Mau grew from fierce social discontent. Perhaps the following figures give a better explanation of Mau Mau in that they show the great contrasts in Kenya in the various standards of living and opportunities to get on in the world:

	Africans	*Indians*	*Europeans*
1. Annual incomes in Kenya 1953:	£27	£280	£660
2. Government money spent per child on primary education 1954:	3s.	18s. 4d.	£49. 6s.

'Uhuru' Is Not Enough

In 1960 the word 'Uhuru' was in common use in East Africa. It was a cry for freedom and independence. Gradually the British government in London recognized African demands for land and a voice in running their own affairs. On the other hand

Jomo Kenyatta and Hastings Banda celebrate the former's release from prison, October 1961

the white settlers were sharply divided. Some accepted that the African majority must eventually rule, but stressed the great prosperity they, the settlers, had brought to Kenya. Others were horrified at the shattering of white control; it seemed to them that far from the Kikuyu seizing independence, the British

A Kenya farm after independence: an African farmer inspects his coffee trees after being awarded a top agricultural prize in Nyanza Province

government were surrendering. These settlers packed up and left, taking much of their considerable wealth with them.

Independence was granted to Kenya on 12 December 1963, despite the fact that the country was in the middle of a land crisis. Of its 140 million acres, only 26 million have the soil quality and rainfall necessary for efficient agriculture. Drought and the tsetse fly control the rest. With the exit of so many white settlers the new Kenya government had to work a minor miracle in land distribution. In three years a start was made: an orderly transfer was made of over a million acres left by or bought from 780 Europeans to 26,000 mostly landless Africans. Without the close government control, a Kenyan has written, 'violence and theft on a large scale' would have resulted.

The leader of this new government was Jomo Kenyatta. Released in 1961, the man who had once been the symbol of witchcraft and hate to the British was free to become Kenya's first prime minister. In a speech on Independence Day he showed he was well aware that the end of colonial rule was not going to answer Kenya's real problems:

'Many people may think that, now there is Uhuru, richness will pour down like manna from heaven. I tell you there will be nothing from heaven. We must all work hard with our hands, to save ourselves from poverty, ignorance and disease.'

13 Congo Tragedy 1960

Recipe for a Contented Colony

At the end of chapter 2 we saw King Leopold handing over his 'personal possession' to the Belgian government in 1908. The memory of what he had done remained. The poet Vachel Lindsay wrote:

> Listen to the yell of Leopold's ghost
> Burning in Hell for his hand-maimed host;
> Hear how the demons chuckle and yell
> Cutting his hands off, down in Hell.

The Belgians were conscious that many other countries were watching their work in the Congo closely. In case these foreigners should find fault the new rulers concentrated on making the Congo prosperous. Its people should earn good money, and have a fair chance of some education, medical services and skilled jobs. In this it was planned that the Congo should develop economically and socially, although it would be governed directly from Brussels. Belgians sincerely believed that it would be many generations before the Congolese were able to govern themselves.

For nearly half a century the Congo was efficiently managed. Belgians did many excellent things there. One of the most important was the development of the country's riches. The copper mines of Katanga, the diamond fields of Kasai, the gold mines of Kivu produced great mineral wealth, and rubber and palm oil production were increased. And the Congo received some share of the profits. King Leopold might claim to have started all this, but his greed had caused terrible human misery.

Belgian ideas were very different. To exploit the minerals there foreign companies were encouraged to invest their money. One of them, the Union Minière of Katanga, grew extremely powerful. Its copper workings were the richest in the world, and slowly other enterprises were added: cobalt and tungsten, hydroelectric power, even the big Sabena airlines. To run all this efficiently it built its own transport system, flour mills and dairies. For Union Minière was not just a company—it could claim to be a miniature welfare state. In the early days it found that many of its African workers only stayed with the Company for a short while before returning to their villages. In order to persuade them to remain in the industrial areas it began offering family housing, free milk, schools and medical care. All this was very attractive to the Africans, and many kinds of people came to work for the Company. It was not an uncommon sight to see a Watutsi of 7 feet 5 inches working in the same road gang as a Pygmy of 4 feet 5 inches.

There were problems. Leopold's agents had forced men to work for them; the Union Minière's agents tempted workers away with offers of prosperity. The result could have been the same: the death through depopulation of many Congolese villages. So the Belgians passed a 'quota' law. A small fixed number of families were allowed to leave each village to work in the mining areas, whilst those who stayed behind had to produce a certain quota of crops, about sixty days' work a year, which the government bought at a fair, fixed price.

The Belgian Mistake

The chances of everyone getting some schooling in the Congo were high. 'We prefer,' said the Belgian Governor-General in 1955, 'to give primary education to the mass of children'. But this was all. There were few secondary schools, and only one university—and that was not opened until 1954. It had twenty-eight students.

If a young man left his village for the town he would find plenty of jobs, ranging from driver's mate and nightwatchman to houseboy, carpenter or mason. If he was successful he might in later years set up as a trader, but his real ambition was to become a clerk or learn a skilled trade. In the 1950s there were many opportunities for this under Belgian rule, and he and his fellows could be seen at work in the mines, in hotels, post offices, airports and as traffic police. The clerks, the 'white-collar workers' were the most respected of these wage-earners: they were called '*evolués*'.

The really able and ambitious Congolese wanted more. The

evolué, having been taken out of his tribal life and given a little education, could see what 'the big city' had to offer. But now he met what was called 'the Line of Rebuff': he was not allowed to join European society and mix socially with the white man as an equal. An American visited the Congo in 1959 and heard many Belgians there speak of 'the fact'—that the natives 'were up in trees just fifty years ago'.

For one *evolué*, proud of the European way of life he felt he was adopting, the supreme insult came whilst he was walking in a European housing area. He turned a corner and accidentally bumped into a white woman. 'Can't you take care, you dirty ape,' she cried. He felt that suddenly all his previous hopes of one day soon taking a place of equality with Europeans were shattered. This man later became the Congo's first prime minister, and was a key figure in the 1960 tragedy. His name was Patrice Lumumba.

Two Leaders

There were therefore no Congolese with an important voice in the government of the Congo. Some African advisers to the Governor-General had been appointed in 1947, but the Belgian intention was made clear in the mid-1950s, when an official statement said, 'Freedom for the Congo in thirty years'. The reaction of educated Congolese was one of despair, because in Brazzaville, just across the River Congo in the French colony General de Gaulle had recently offered independence to French subjects there as soon as they wanted. Feelings on the subject ran high in the Congolese towns; late in 1958 rioting broke out in Leopoldville in which forty-nine Africans died.

At this point two men emerged as leaders of the Congolese. Patrice Lumumba, in his early thirties, was a tall, bony, slightly stooping ex-brewery salesman. He was a fine public speaker who could hold the attention of a throng of people. He read a great deal, and a friend of his recorded that on his bookshelves were a wide variety of authors—Voltaire, the eighteenth-century philosopher, Winston Churchill, and the detective-story writer Agatha Christie. He and his party stood for a united independent Congo. But they made wild promises: more money, cars, plenty of work or, if they thought it would appeal to their listeners, no work at all! One Lumumba supporter carried a large, coloured photograph of an American skyscraper with him, and he promised that after independence all village huts would be replaced by the one in the photograph.

Lumumba's rival was Joseph Kasavubu. An older man by ten years, he was shy and spoke softly in a rambling way. In appearance also he was far from the hero type: small, plump-faced with thick glasses. He passionately wanted his own people of the Ba-Kongo—one million of them—to have their own government. So he supported a federation, a loose union of the different Congo peoples, each having its own ruler.

The Belgians became alarmed as support for these two men grew throughout 1958 and 1959. The rioting was so unexpected. What they feared most was a long and costly colonial war like the Algerian one. So they gave way to Congolese demands for negotiations about the Congo's future.

Disaster 1960

In January 1960 a Round Table Conference took place in Ostend, Belgium. African leaders, who left the Congo to attend the talks, said later that the most they hoped for was independence in about five years. But the Belgian government and public panicked. Stories spread about the high cost of keeping law and order in the Congo. 'Not a single soldier to the Congo' was a Brussels newspaper headline. In the light of this attitude the Conference set the date for independence: 30 June 1960. This was only six months away!

Within that time, not only had Lumumba and Kasavubu to settle their differences, but also all the important positions in the country had to be handed over—government posts, taxation officials, judges, doctors. But to whom? There was no trained African civil service; only seventeen Congolese had ever graduated from a university; there were no doctors at all until two were due to finish their studies in 1961. Independence would be a sham if the new state had to rely completely on Europeans to run things.

This was not all. When Independence Day arrived the new Congolese government checked their country's financial resources, and found it *owed* Belgium £15 million. Yet the annual Congolese revenue from exports had been £1,000 million. Also, a £70 million gold reserve figure which had been published in 1958 had fallen to £3½ million in 1960. The Belgians explained some of this away by saying that their officials needed pensions. Obviously, also, the Belgian settlers and industrialists had withdrawn much of the capital they had invested in the Congo.

At least Lumumba and Kasavubu had patched up their dis-agreements. One was to be prime minister and the other president. King Baudouin of Belgium went to the Congo for the independence celebrations, and spoke in praise of the great things Belgians had done for the country. Lumumba was very rude to him. 'We are no longer your monkeys', he shouted at the king.

Disaster struck the Congo on the fifth day of independence. The 23,000-strong Congolese Army, which still had white Belgian officers, mutinied, because its generals had refused to promote any Africans to the rank of officer. Destruction was widespread, and white officers and their wives were attacked, killed or imprisoned. European civilians began leaving the Congo in their thousands: Leopoldville airport was compared by one reporter to 'a battlefield'. Soon law and order through-out the country broke down completely.

Belgian troops were hastily flown in to protect European property and lives, but this only made the tension worse. In Kasai Province in the interior tribal warfare broke out and thousands died in bloodthirsty atrocities. Amidst this confusion a new figure appeared on the scene. In Katanga, the rich copper province, Moise Tshombe on 11 July declared his 'state' independent of the Congo.

With foreign troops on his soil and the country falling to pieces, Lumumba appealed the next day to the United Nations for help. This came very quickly in the form of a peace-keeping force, but Lumumba clearly expected the UN now to invade Katanga and compel Tshombe to accept the authority of the Congo government. When the UN refused Lumumba appealed abroad again—this time to Soviet Russia. In August 1960 Soviet technicians and nineteen big Illyushin planes arrived to help in a massive Congolese drive on Katanga. It failed.

Chaos in the Congo was now complete.

The Struggle for Power

Calling in the Russians was Lumumba's great error. There were too many individuals and groups competing for power already. In a desperate attempt to settle the country the Congolese Army, with new African officers under Colonel Mobutu, seized control of the government. The Russians were ordered out, and Lumumba arrested whilst fleeing from the capital. He was flown to Katanga for imprisonment by his worst enemy, Tshombe. In February 1961 he died there in mysterious circumstances.

It was soon clear that Mobutu's government would be bankrupt without the mineral wealth of Katanga. In an effort to

The man-in-the-street's unconcern for the difficulties of the United Nations forces in the Congo 1960

preserve the country's unity, the United Nations agreed to do what Lumumba had originally wanted: force Katanga back into the Congo State. For two years the world and especially the other new African nations watched the unhappy sight of a 10,000-strong UN Force and its jet planes struggle with Tshombe's well-armed and well-disciplined Katangese Army. This army, backed by Union Minière funds, was officered by white mercenaries—soldiers of fortune who were known as 'Les Affreux', the Frightful Ones.

The UN won, but at a price. Tshombe, perhaps the most hated man in Black Africa, was nevertheless so influential and powerful that his rule over the whole Congo was accepted by the United Nations in 1964. Tshombe was a big, six-foot tall, burly figure, and his speeches show that he had a shrewd mind. With great energy he set about clearing up the confusion. But his reliance on foreign support left him a very unpopular man. Within a year Mobutu was back in control, and Tshombe overthrown and in exile. Although his enemy was now out of the way, Mobutu still had to solve the problem of Katanga. In 1967 he provided his answer: refusing to share profits with the Union Minière, he seized total control of the Company. He lost a great deal of world sympathy for this action, but he has nevertheless kept a precarious control.

Perhaps it has been the Congo's tragedy that, since Lumumba's death, the two ablest men in the country, Tshombe the politician and Mobutu the soldier, have been unable to work together.

14 Rhodesian Jigsaw

The Legacy of Cecil Rhodes

Rhodes died of a heart disease in 1902. More than any other man he could claim to have 'created' the country in central Africa which white settlers called Rhodesia.

With the Royal Charter granted in 1889 to his British South Africa Company (the BSA) he had claimed to rule over a huge, but vague area north of the River Limpopo. The British government during the partition period of 1885–95 had settled the outer boundaries: with Leopold's Congo to the north-west, Portuguese Mozambique to the east, and German East Africa to the north-east. Rhodes wanted total Company control throughout this area. Company authority was accepted in the Salisbury-Bulawayo region, but around Lake Nyasa he faced opposition from a Scottish-financed Lakes Company and from the man who had fought to keep Nyasaland out of Portuguese hands—Harry Johnstone. The British government eventually created a protectorate over it. To the north of the Zambezi River he was more successful, but there were other difficulties. It was a harsh country, and a number of early settlers died from malaria. 'The future of Northern Rhodesia lies in the quinine bottle,' said one medical officer.

Rhodes's idea of a single Rhodesia just would not work. For one thing the many peoples of the area had different ways of life and background. The white settlers were only the latest 'tribe' to move in. For another the great Zambezi valley, which cuts in two the 5,000 feet high plateau of south-central Africa, was like a frontier. Most white settlers stayed south of the river where the land and climate were more suited to them. To the north were African peoples, whose development, unlike those to the south, had been more affected by Arab traders and slavers and later by Christian missionaries.

So, beginning in 1923, when the British government ended BSA Company control, the area was clearly divided into three parts: Southern Rhodesia, Northern Rhodesia and Nyasaland.

Southern Rhodesia was given the choice of joining the Union of South Africa or of becoming a self-governing British colony. Only big property owners could vote, and this meant the white settlers. They chose the second. They had their own government now, with their own parliament, police and armed forces. The British in London controlled only two things: foreign policy and a tiny but important power to watch how Black Rhodesians were treated.

North of the Zambezi the British Colonial Office established control over the two protectorates of Northern Rhodesia and Nyasaland. Here the interests of the Black Africans were accepted as being most important—'paramountcy' it was called—because of the small number of white settlers (6,000). To the south real power rested with the 35,000 whites.

Rhodes had failed his settlers in two ways. He had not gained part of Mozambique to give his 'colony' an outlet to the sea, and his hope that there was another goldfield near Salisbury as rich as the Rand was not fulfilled.

Mines, Railways and Farms

In the 1920s and 1930s the future of the three territories depended on how prosperous they could make themselves. The settlers were energetic, ambitious and well able to exploit the natural resources of the area. With the annual production of gold in Rhodesia in the early years of the century only worth £3½ million, it was obvious that the gold dream had come to an end. Men turned to other activities. Coal was found at Wankie in 1903 and later investigations proved the resources to be one of the world's biggest. Poor quality surface copper was also found about the same time in Northern Rhodesia; later, deep-mining probes revealed the riches of the great Copper Belt. The copper boom began in the 1920s. From exports of £½ million the figure rose in the next thirty years to £82 million.

Mining was difficult in the early years because of the lack of good transportation. This led to the extension of a railway network from the Union of South Africa into the three territories. This railway had to pay for itself, so it only went to places which produced goods for export. Nyasaland suffered from this, especially its unproductive northern areas.

With the railway came more settlers to all the territories. They stayed close to the line for the easy marketing of their goods. In the south beef cattle and maize became important products; tobacco was also grown, but it was not of very good quality until after 1904 when some American seed was used and a special indoor process, called 'flue-curing', was introduced. In 1910 the Rhodesian Tobacco Planters' Association was formed in Salisbury, and the first tobacco auction sales were held. These men were the forerunners of what soon became a powerful, prosperous white farming community.

White settlers and their government in Salisbury brought European industrial organization to replace the great African kingdoms which had once ruled the vast plateau for generations. Roads, dams and bridges; copper and coal mines; acres of land covered with maize and tobacco; modern towns: these brought prosperity to Rhodesia.

To the black African the introduction into his country of a European way of life was revolutionary. The mines, railways and big farms needed a labour force, and the colonial government needed taxes. It was therefore doubly convenient for the white settlers that Africans had to seek work with them in order to earn wages to pay the taxes. Not all of them accepted such a change without resistance. Although a hut tax was fixed as early as 1894 at £1 a year with an extra 10*s.* for each wife after the first, even a generation later many Africans were unwilling to work permanently as labourers. They left the farms and mines in the wet season to return home to plough their family land.

This exasperated the settlers, whose continued prosperity

A tobacco auction in Salisbury, Rhodesia.

depended on knowing they had a regular, constant supply of workers. So, in Southern Rhodesia, two things were introduced in the 1930s to defend what Godfrey Huggins, premier of the country, called 'a white island of civilization in a sea of black barbarism'. First, in 1931, a Land Act was passed. The Southern Rhodesian government was convinced that the majority of Africans would take a long time to accept the changes going on around them. So 'points of contact,' said a report, 'should be reduced until the native has advanced very much further on the paths of civilization'. By the Act 'Europeans' had to stay on their 49 million acres, 'Natives' on their 29 million acres and another 18 million acres were to be divided later. To the European way of thinking such an arrangement prevented rivalry between the races over land purchase, and most 'European' land was on the red soils of the high veld, which was difficult to work without modern, expensive ploughs.

Secondly Pass Laws which had been introduced by the BSA Company in 1894 were confirmed by the Southern Rhodesian government in 1936. For the white settlers these meant they could keep track of Africans who moved from job to job and then back home again, by insisting that they carried identity cards. If some Africans were unhappy about the way the Land Act had been worked out, they were clear in their minds that the Pass Laws meant racial discrimination, for without these passes they could not get well-paid jobs.

North of the Zambezi the British government did not force such 'segregation' on the people. There were still many men coming from the Lake Nyasa region to work for periods of two or three years in the Copper Belt and then returning home; others coming to stay, bringing their families with them to live in the industrial towns. Here they learned European ways and envied European wealth. In Nyasaland, 'the beautiful but poor Cinderella colony', the experience of 'going away' to work for the white man produced much unease. 'There is no respect like there is in our country,' said one African chief. In this can be found the seeds of the national movement for independence.

Federation 1953

During the Second World War 10,000 people of all races from the three territories went on military service to Europe and to

India. Africans returned in 1945 with high hopes of improved job opportunities. The demand by Britain for wartime products had brought on an industrial revolution in the Rhodesias. After 1945 new white settlers also poured in: 16,000 a year by 1950.

With economic progress and an expanding population it was obviously time to reconsider the colonial organization, and the old Rhodes ideal of a unified, progressive area was revived. One suggestion was that all three territories should be merged into a single nation. But Britain insisted on a federation. This would ensure that each territory could develop in its own time —otherwise the more advanced Southern Rhodesia would dominate the other two. With federation they should cooperate closely on road and rail construction, medical research, and perhaps the biggest need, hydroelectric power. For the great Kariba Dam across the Zambezi was already being planned.

To the British, federation seemed the positive solution. The old Rhodes area had fallen apart in the early twentieth century like pieces of a jigsaw. Federation would fit them together again into a combination which must result in a higher standard of living for all. A further argument in the British government's eyes was that a loyal, prosperous and large Commonwealth Dominion astride one of Africa's biggest rivers would offset the Boer Nationalist power that was growing to the south (see chapter 20).

A conference met at Victoria Falls in 1949 to work out the details, and in October 1953 the Federation was set up. Nevertheless even after the four years of negotiations the black Africans of Northern Rhodesia and Nyasaland were suspicious: the old 'paramountcy' was in danger and African interests might be ignored. Two remarks by leading white figures in the Federation, Sir Godfrey Huggins and Sir Roy Welensky, alarmed the blacks. Huggins wrote in 1956: 'Political control must remain in the hands of civilized people, which for the foreseeable future means the Europeans.' His ideas had not changed since the 1930s. And when Welensky called the Federation a 'rider and a horse', the African knew very well that he was the horse! Nor was the prosperity promised to the African quick to come—in 1961 the average European wage-earner had £1,200 a year; the African £87.

Violence in Nyasaland

Dissatisfaction grew most quickly in Nyasaland. Here white settlers were few, because the Lake shores and the immediate area around were heavily populated with Yao and other African peoples, and there were no easy mining opportunities. By the mid-twentieth century many African men were travelling outside their own homeland to the Copper Belt of Northern Rhodesia, where they were an essential part of the labour force, living in camps, apart from their families. For them Federation offered nothing.

In July 1958 Dr Hastings Banda returned to Nyasaland. He had been away many years practising as a doctor in London and the Gold Coast, but he had kept in close touch with the opinions of his fellow Africans. He was one of a group who for a long time had declared, 'Our goal is African self-government'. Banda led a whirlwind campaign whose catch-phrase was 'To Hell with Federation'. Tension in the country increased. In March 1959 the British Governor feared for law and order and declared a state of emergency. Violence broke out, and at Nkata Bay on Lake Nyasa twenty Africans were killed by police; 1,346 arrests were made, and half of them, including Banda, stayed in prison for a year.

The Africans had made their point. The British sent investigators to Nyasaland; they returned to London convinced that African opposition to Federation was 'deeply rooted'. The whole idea of Federation was immediately questioned in the Westminster Parliament. Lord Monckton went to Rhodesia on behalf of the British government and wrote later, 'For the African the partnership is a sham.'

Both Hastings Banda in Nyasaland and Kenneth Kaunda in Northern Rhodesia quickly seized on this change in British opinion. They asked if they could take their countries out of the Federation. Within two years arrangements were completed: The Rhodesian jigsaw once more broke up. In 1964 Nyasaland became the independent state of Malawi (named after the old sixteenth century African kingdom), and Northern Rhodesia took the name Zambia. Voting for a government in these new nations was the right of every adult, and as black voters outnumbered white, no white settlers had any direct control in the two governments north of the Zambezi.

U.D.I.

The government in Salisbury which had tried to keep the Federation together found itself the target of much criticism from white settlers who were relieved that 'the black north had cut itself adrift'. A new government was formed under Winston Field. He and his supporters wanted total independence for Southern Rhodesia, with the old Rhodes ideal of 'civilized men' in control. The British knew this meant in practice denying the right of an equal vote to the majority of black Rhodesians, and by the 1923 Clause (see page 99) Britain refused in all negotiations to grant independence.

By the spring of 1964 even Field found himself too moderate for most white Rhodesians. There were other solutions than the continuing round of talks. A precise, immediate answer—UDI, a unilateral declaration of independence—was suggested by one man. Rhodesia, he said, would take independence like the American colonists had done in 1776, despite Britain's warning that it would be 'an illegal act of rebellion'. This man was Ian Smith. He forced Field out of power, and on 11 November 1965 UDI was announced.

A worldwide crisis took place. Smith claimed the right of 250,000 white men to rule over 4 million black men. He said Salisbury, not London, should decide when and where Africans were 'civilized', and thus ready to vote. Although she refused to send troops to quell the Rhodesian 'rebellion' as some of the black African states wanted, Britain agreed to take the issue to the United Nations. Here sanctions were imposed, and many essential supplies, normally sent to Rhodesia from the rest of the world, were cut off. In the four years since UDI these sanctions have not succeeded in changing the policy of the Smith government. Discussions in Salisbury and between Ian Smith and the British prime minister, Harold Wilson aboard the warships *Tiger* in 1966 and *Fearless* in 1968 have all been deadlocked on the issue of how soon Africans shall have equal voting rights.

Looking back over the independence movements since 1945, one clear dividing line has come into existence: the River Zambezi. To the north, Arab and black governments rule; to the south white control remains.

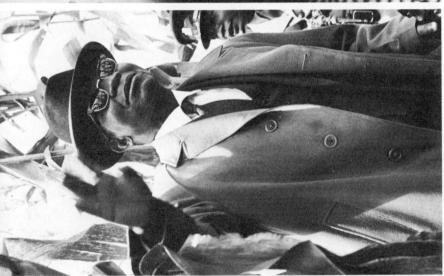

Katangan and Congolese statesman

Above centre: Patrice Lumumba, the tragic first premier of the Congo Republic

Above right: Colonel Nasser, a photograph taken about 1952

Right: Dr Hastings Banda, Nyasaland and Malawi statesman

Far right: Nelson Mandela, the Black Pimpernel

15 Who Governs and How?

How to Be 'Modern'

A novelist from Malawi, David Rubadiri, wrote in 1967: 'The African is in the midst of the turmoil of making sense with what has hit him for the last one hundred years.'

The key year seemed to be 1960. The movements to independence that so greatly changed the political map of Africa were gathering strength. The British recognized this when Prime Minister Harold Macmillan made a speech in Cape Town: 'The wind of change is blowing through this continent, and whether we like it or not this growth of national consciousness is a political fact.'

Huge areas of Africa followed Ghana's example and gained independence without bloodshed. It is worth noting that only in colonies with white settlers were prolonged disputes or fighting necessary—in Rhodesia, Algeria and Kenya; whereas the civil wars in the Congo, Nigeria and Sudan occurred *after* independence.

The new governments had much in their favour. As Europeans left there was plenty of promotion. Most of the new leaders had the good wishes of the ex-colonial power. More than anything there was the enthusiasm—the feeling about a country that 'it is ours'.

The new African rulers did not wish to return to the old ways before the Europeans came. They had seen enough of the benefits of industrial and commercial civilization to want them for themselves. In short they wished to be modern. Yet many Africans expected too much from independence. It did not take them long to realize that their freedom was only political. As far as their desire for prosperity was concerned they still had to turn to the ex-colonial powers for help, for they were still economically dependent. In the next chapters we shall look at the social and economic difficulties of the new African countries; but first a glance at the politicians. What kind of people were they, and what kinds of questions did they have to answer?

The New Ruling Elite

The ambitions of those who took over from the colonial governments are easily stated: to create an African society based on
the rights of man—the right to take part in one's country's
government; the personal freedoms of worship, speech, travel,
ownership of property and fair trial; the right to good food,
housing, education and medical care. To the ruling élite, the
politicians, doctors, teachers, civil servants, nurses, this is what
being 'modern' meant.

These ambitions were not so easy to achieve. Large numbers
of people were still living in the traditional ways. Even today,
how to get them to change is still Africa's greatest task.

Following independence the new African rulers retained
such democratic methods of government as voting for representatives, who then formed different political parties in a
country's parliament. They realized that modern ways would
only be introduced slowly, after much discussion and explanation. An expert on African affairs has written, 'Unlike the
revolutionary leaders like Stalin and Mao in Russia and China,
they did not propose to drag the peasants screaming into the
twentieth century.' By the mid-1960s the seizures of power by
army officers showed that peaceful, democratic solutions had
failed in places.

What Went Wrong? Some Answers

Europeans have said, 'Oh well, what do you expect? The
Africans are too tribal.' Or, 'Look at Nkrumah and Ben Bella—
they were corrupted by power.' The answers are more complicated than these easily-arrived-at conclusions indicate. In fact,
some writers, sympathetic to African difficulties, have remarked
that life is changing so rapidly there that it is a wonder there
have not been more Congos and Nigerias.

The clash of old and new is a much better description of the
situation. A Nigerian writer put it this way: 'We were in the
rain until yesterday [Independence Day]; then a handful of us,
smart and lucky ones, scrambled for the one shelter the former
rulers left and barricaded ourselves in.' These were the new
ruling élite who, in the rush to take over modern standards,
seemed to have forgotten their less advanced brothers. Another
writer, the Malawian, Dunduza Chisiza, warned this élite 'not

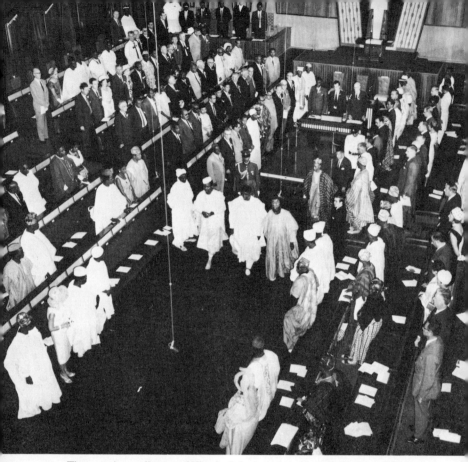

The sovereign parliament of Nigeria. It looks and works much like its model, the British parliament at Westminster

to imitate foreigners' in displaying their wealth; otherwise the ordinary people of Africa would feel that their country had been taken over, and that 'white Europeans' had merely been replaced by 'black Europeans'. In keeping on the urban-centred administrations they had inherited, many of the new rulers had to live in towns. Soon they lost contact and sympathy with the villagers they seemed to have little time to visit. An investigator in Nigeria heard nasty references being made to 'those illiterates' of the out-of-town areas. These two groups, the modern élite with its western style of life and the traditional African villager, have been well-described by Guy Hunter: he called them the 'Chevrolet society and the bicycle society'.

It is not just a matter of money. An African who left his

village to visit Europe or North America on an education scholarship is called 'a Been-to'. Abroad he has seen all the advantages of an advanced town society and he returns home full of enthusiasm for change; he finds, sadly, that the people he left behind have not moved in their ideas at all. He may arrive in his large car, looking very smart in his western-style suit. He finds he is looked up to as the shining example for the youths of the village. But the chances of many of them reaching the top of the ladder are extremely small, and hopes are often shattered after much time, money and effort have been spent. There are not enough schools and teachers—or even jobs—yet. So the politicians are both envied for their good fortune, and blamed for not providing others with immediate opportunities.

What Kind of Government?

Here and there were Africans who decided that the effort to modernize was not worth it, or that the old tribal ways were best. A poet wrote, feelingly, 'I would go back to darkness and peace.' Others, like Frantz Fanon, launched a biting attack on the élite. 'Political freedom unaccompanied by social revolution is a sham and a snare', he wrote in his book, *The Wretched of the Earth*, which has become the bible of African socialists. They see the first duty of a government as looking after the welfare of the ordinary people.

One leader took his new country out of west European influence altogether. 'We prefer poverty in freedom to riches in slavery,' said the leader of ex-French Guinea, Sékou Touré. The French were so angry at his socialist ideas that they removed all their equipment when they left, even the telephones and the typewriters. Touré appealed to the Russians and Chinese for aid. With the Congo example in mind, African leaders feared that their continent might become a Cold War battlefield. Dr Hastings Banda of Malawi pleaded with the other new nations not to launch 'a second scramble for the soul of Africa' between the Western world and the Communist powers.

At independence many Africans were given the vote, although they had little formal education. They were not used to the complex system of party organization, policies and all the paraphernalia of regular elections. So they tended to identify

Africa 1970. With dates of independence from European rule

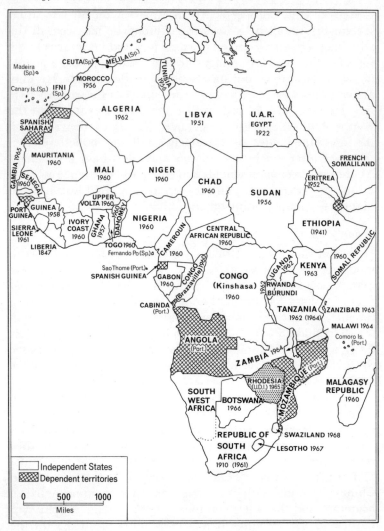

themselves with a particular person, sometimes an army general (such as Mobutu) or a 'party boss' (Nkrumah).

One difficulty is the word 'opposition'. Some Africans do not think the idea of an official opposition, like the one Britain has, will work in Africa. To them it does not mean an alternative government. For instance, 'opposition' in Swahili can also be translated as 'enmity', and in other African languages it means 'hooligans' or 'sabotage'.

A second difficulty is that of the minorities. During the partition period many boundaries were just straight lines drawn on a blank map. The result of this has been that the new nations of Africa are made up of peoples differing widely in their language, religion, physical appearance and prosperity. Some are minorities who object strongly to being ruled by other 'races'. We have seen how Katanga tried to secede, or break away, from the Congo Republic; the Ibo people tried to do the same in Nigeria in the late 1960s, setting up their own state of Biafra. In the civil war that followed in Biafra the rights and wrongs of Africa's biggest political question were fought out. Has each 'people', 'nation' or 'tribe' the right to form its own government? If so, Africa could well have 200 states. Or should states be federations large enough to compete in world markets, stand equal with world powers and organize big welfare services?

Unity

It is unlikely that the present map of Africa will remain the same. What Africans mistook for independence was only stage one: freedom from foreign rule. The 1960s have seen attempts to answer questions like: what boundaries, and what form of government? The answers are not final.

Some people have argued that it was not 'nationalism' that took the new nations to independence; it was 'Africanism'. So men like Nkrumah wanted some kind of united Africa. This movement is called Pan-Africanism, and in 1963 the OAU (Organization for African Unity) was set up. But today its members are far from united and none is willing to trust his country to the presidency of someone like Nkrumah. Countries cooperating in trading groups look like having more success in 1970 (see chapter 18).

16 The Old and the New in Rural Africa

Kith and Kin

For generations an African's 'relationships', how he behaved and got on with other people, were always more important than what he owned or was (i.e. his property and status). And the most important relationships were those of the family. But 'family' has two meanings. In the modern industrialized countries of western Europe and North America it is a small group called the nuclear family: a man, his wife and young children who often moved about from job to job and place to place. In African society the family is regarded as a much larger unit, and is called an extended family which includes distant cousins, aunts and uncles and grandparents, all of whom live close together in a compound or village. A traditional Yoruba compound of south Nigeria, for instance, may have a thousand persons in it. Here life is close-knit and friendly, with its frequent celebrations and rounds of visits to your kith and kin.

An extended family is, however, much more than this. A member is expected to be loyal to the group, and his individual ambitions must be those of the family. If he gives this loyalty the group will look after him when he is old or crippled. Also if a man left the village for a while to seek work in a town, he could always return if unemployed. The European managers of a Northern Rhodesian coal-mine were amazed when, in the 1931 slump, they dismissed 7,000 African workers; all of them just melted away, back to the villages and relatives.

Who owns the land is a vital feature of African family relationships. Here again the modern westerners and the rural Africans have different ideas. To the first land is a 'thing', to be plotted precisely on a map, cut into pieces and each parcel of land bought and sold on the market. To the second, as a Nigerian chief once said, 'land belongs to a large family, some of whose members are dead, some are living and innumerable others as yet unborn'. This land is not split up permanently into pieces at all—with nomadic groups this would be impossible anyway.

What happens is this: the chief of an area or council of elders of a tribe take a large, often indefinite, piece of land around some traditional point like a shrine or well, and allot a certain amount—about two to three acres—to each nuclear family. If an individual member of a family clears part of the forest or savannah, he has full rights to this—but only during the normal period of cultivation. When it is left to fallow his rights end. Thus, for nomadic tribes like the Fulani or Bedouin Arabs the position of a man's farm varies from one crop rotation to another. For tribes who do not practise such shifting cultivation group rights still apply. A man claims as much land as his family can use, but should he fail to make full use of any part of this land it is allocated to others.

Although a man does not *own* his land, he can claim it as a birthright and it gives him security. To the rural African, says one writer, 'his kinship group was his insurance society, his old age pension, his community'.

Farming

Two phrases have been used to describe African country life in the past: 'primitive in the extreme' and 'subsistence farming'. The first is how a westerner compares Africa to his own experience, and the second is a phrase for a rural society which produces food for a group's own use and not for sale at a market. Although much African farming in the 1960s is still far from efficient or scientific, neither of these phrases is accurate today.

To western eyes, one observer said, an old African farm is 'a riot of vegetation, grasses, cassava and maize shooting up together and pumpkin vines trailing across a pathway'. Its fields look like small, odd-shaped patches in the bush, which has not been properly cleared of roots because of the crude axes and knives used. There are also many tall forest trees scattered about a field—it seems no one has bothered to cut them down.

Yet this is not as inefficient and disorderly as it appears. Tropical African soils are light and do not have much plant food in them. The heat and heavy rains rid the top soil of important minerals which crops need; on some slopes the soil can be washed away altogether. This process, called soil erosion, is an all-important problem in African farming. Both the smallness of a field and the 'riot of vegetation' help conserve the soil, and the constant green canopy of trees over the land reduces the damage of rain and sun.

There remains much wrong with the old methods. Insufficient food of the right kind is produced; pests are numerous and vary from baboons to locusts, the mealy-bug and white ants; brush-fires, in which tall savannah grass is burnt off for second-cropping, makes soil erosion worse. Experts from the industrialized western countries who advise the new African nations think that much of this can be put right: the knowledge is there, they say, but people have to be persuaded. Educated Africans advise caution. They think massive changes on western lines will produce social discontent.

The people who are most likely to accept fresh, scientific ideas in farming are the younger generation. But here lies the really difficult problem of rural Africa: the way the ambitious and energetic young men are leaving the countryside for the towns.

'*The Wants*'

In a story entitled *Trial by Sasswood*, set in Liberia some years ago, a character complains that many Africans are catching that terrible, wasting disease of Europeans, 'the Wants'. This is the growing desire for some things which only money can buy —material goods such as radios, bicycles and shirts. Cash is needed, so either a new crop for sale in a market or export abroad (like cocoa in West Africa) must be introduced; or men must travel to the towns or the few big European-owned farms for jobs. A move to the town need not be permanent; more often it is a seasonal 'labour migration'. For some Africans this involves travelling on foot, 200 miles or so. Hausa people do this from Sokoto in northern Nigeria to the tin mines at Jos or even to Ibadan or Lagos.

In this way Africans try to maintain two occupations: a trading or factory job for the men, whilst the women keep a small farm going. It has its advantages in that it gets cash and material goods into the villages, which in turn makes those who have remained seek ways of raising their standard of living. But the long separation of husband and wife during the 'migration' can break up a family. And doubling up of occupations sometimes results in neither job being done well. An investigation

A machine for making cassava flour being worked alongside the old method

into a 'cocoa migrant' in Ghana found that he could only save about £10 for a season's work. He spent most of this on gifts for his relatives—a bicycle and some cloth. Yet the bicycle was soon pawned or sold to buy seed for a new crop, so the local community gained little permanent advantage from the extra cash-work done.

The Right Kind of Change

Clearly the best solution is to make rural life more attractive and profitable. How to do it will be one of Africa's big questions of the 1970s. Efforts have been made in the 1950s and 1960s; some have failed and others promise a great deal. Experience shows that three things are fundamental. First, if new tools are needed they must not be big and expensive. What one critic called the 'shiny red tractor mentality' led to much wasted effort in the 1950s. It was found that a tractor in parts of Africa actually increased soil erosion; also that a tractor-plough is valueless if it clears twenty acres when a farmer can only weed four with his hoe; further, who repairs the tractor when it breaks down? Secondly, in some places much patient explanation is needed if the required changes in land ownership are to be made. Thirdly, the cash return for adopting a new method of farming must be seen to be well worth the extra work often involved.

Even big schemes have gone wrong. The British government planned a groundnuts scheme in south-east Tanganyika just

117

after the Second World War. The area proved too dry, and clearing the scrub and trees too expensive. In 1951, after £35 million had been spent, it was abandoned.

But small-scale and patient improvement further north brought important changes to the Chagga and Kikuyu peoples. In October 1966 a particular farm was investigated. Its owner told of his father who, back in the 1930s, had grown only maize and bananas, and had made £20 cash income a year. Yet in 1966 the farm was a 10 acre smallholding, of which two acres were specially tended for coffee and maize, and half-an-acre was set aside for tomatoes; five good quality dairy cattle were also grazed—they gave four gallons of milk daily. The farmer had recently bought a diesel pump to ease the problem of getting water from a stream for the cattle. He marketed his produce for £750 each year.

Another example from Zambia shows how scientific fish-farming was introduced. Zambia has no coastline, but its rivers were dammed to create eight fish ponds. Measurements were taken, and in one acre 200 lb of fish were put in. Left to themselves a year later there were 600 lb of fish in it; fed with a special cheap food, meliebran, the same acre produced 3,000 lb of fish. Thus at a cost of one penny a lb this scheme provides a cheap source of protein for the Zambian population.

The People of Bamenda, Cameroon

In the highlands of Cameroon is an area which is a good illustration of the problems Africans meet when the traditional methods of farming change to the modern. The Bamenda Highlands rise to a plateau 4,000 feet above the dense tropical forests. Access is difficult: a poor road from Nigeria becomes sticky mud in the 100 inches of rain annually. The Highlands themselves have great advantages—deep, fertile and well-drained volcanic soil and good grazing land out of reach of the tsetse-fly which kills off animals in lower-lying tropical regions.

The people of Bamenda are of very mixed stock, consisting of West African Negroes, some Bantu-speaking tribes from central Africa and the nomadic Fulani people. In the last quarter of a century contacts with new ideas and the influence of education have been slowly changing the traditional sub-sistence agriculture. The Arabica Coffee plant was successfully

An expert from a UNO Agency sharing out chemical fertilizer in the Congo

brought in after the Second World War, and the 14 tons of coffee produced in 1947 had increased to 2,000 tons in 1966. Tea is a recent venture, and the Irish potato grows well in the cool, rainy climate.

These changes created difficulties. The best land for cropping is in the valleys of the Highlands. The new crop, coffee, required more land, which could only be obtained by going up the slopes —and soil erosion is a serious risk at an angle of 35 degrees. As coffee farming is a man's job and he argues that as a cash-crop it must have the best soils of the lower slopes, the women become discontented when they found they were forced to cultivate *their* food crops up on the steeper sides of the valleys.

The second problem is the tension between the farmers and the Fulani nomads. The latter are some 10,000 herdsmen owning about a $\frac{1}{4}$ million cattle, and as the Bamenda arable farmers move up the valley slopes they trespass on the traditional grazing land of the Fulani.

Again these herdsmen have been difficult to tempt into using modern, progressive methods of farming. They do not like selling their cattle, because, as in many parts of Africa, cows are a symbol of wealth and status. But like everyone else the Fulani have to pay taxes to the Cameroon government, so a meat scheme was put into operation in 1958 to bring in good cash returns for the Fulani. Cattle sold at tax time were specially fattened, slaughtered and frozen for quick sale in the neighbouring Nigerian markets. It worked well for three years, until in 1961 Cameroon became independent. Immediately Nigeria imposed a 50 per cent import duty on meat and the scheme became unprofitable. Independence clearly had its drawbacks! (See Map on page 69.)

17 ...And He Came to a City

The Need for Change

We saw in the last chapter that the African way of life had been for centuries a rural one. This has been well described as 'a village civilization'. The few African towns were colourful, noisy markets; here local goods were exchanged: hoes for yams, pots for bananas, cotton cloth for cassava. In time these markets attracted products from great distances: Chinese porcelain, magnificent wheel-made Persian pottery, cloths of India. But urban life in a city is something new in Africa, and it came with the Europeans who brought their civilization of machines and factories.

Most African peoples are still villagers at heart. Was this old, unrushed way of life happier than today? Many Africans have remarked that the cooperation of the villages offered something better than the 'harsh man-against-man competition of modern times'. A Ghanaian poet, Dei Anang, wrote:

Here we stand,
Poised between two civilizations;
Backward? To the days of the drum
And festal dances in the shade,
Of sun-kist palms;
Or forward?
Forward!
Toward?
The slums, where man is dumped on man
The factory
To grind hard hours
In an inhuman mill
In one long ceaseless spell.

Other Africans argued that Africa must keep pace with the modern western world. This meant adopting new methods of producing goods, using machinery and scientific ideas. The old handicraft methods, they said, would not do. But two things

Working in the copper belt of Zambia

prevented widespread change until the mid-twentieth century. First, there were the strong traditions of Africa which taught that one should 'tread in the steps of one's ancestors', and that a good man must live as his neighbour lived—not worse, but also not much better. The second was the attitude of the colonial powers.

The Colonial Legacy

Europeans brought to Africa their own ideas on progress. They created roads and cities, and they introduced novel methods of teaching and keeping law and order. At the start it was thought these would modernize Africa; time, though, revealed serious drawbacks. A tarmac road did not by itself create traffic and an exchange of goods. And educating people did not necessarily make them enterprising and businesslike.

The colonial answer to the question of making Africa prosperous was twofold: mine its valuable minerals, and grow crops which were needed abroad and could be exported easily from ports at the mouths of the big rivers. In some areas the answer worked well. In the copper mines of Katanga and Northern Rhodesia (Zambia); with the cocoa-farmers of the Gold Coast (Ghana) and with the Kikuyu coffee-growers of Kenya a higher standard of living resulted. But all this depended on European technology (what Americans call 'know-how') and European money.

There was little attempt to foster African skills. This, perhaps, was the most disastrous feature of colonial rule. Economists tell us that for 'development' to occur, it is essential that a man should take a raw material, work on it with skill and so add value to it, then sell the finished product. The prosperity of many of the rich nations of the world has been built on this principle, with machine power added. In Africa, however, some curious things happened during colonial rule. One country exported raw timber, sisal and hides; and imported furniture, rope and shoes. A few imaginative District Commissioners might use local labour to develop a new crop or a small irrigation scheme. In general, though, the colonial legacy was what one expert has called 'outlandish rather than native'. This means that the effort, skill and initiative in industry was foreign, not African.

With the rush for independence the emergent nations of Africa wanted to catch-up with the western world. The new rulers, the élite class, many of whom had been educated in Europe or America, felt this most strongly. They wished to transfer what was 'modern' to Africa, and this included technology, ideas, values and institutions. In many places, however, the speed of change produced the opposite of what Africans wanted.

Africa: a Continent in a Hurry

Machine-powered industry seemed the solution to African backwardness. This was how Africa would modernize. Now, a modern factory needs a regular supply of the right kind of raw

The Kariba Dam on the Zambian-Rhodesian frontier. The wall is 420 feet high and the lake stretches behind it for 175 miles

materials; money (capital) to buy them; managers who know about mass-production and book-keeping on a large scale; workmen who are trained, careful and used to the fixed hours of factory life; power to work the machines; and finally salesmen and a good market in which to sell goods. It took Europe over a century to industrialize and balance all the complexities. The nations of Africa wanted to do it immediately and spectacularly.

The difficulties were enormous. Attempts were made to set up industries like flour-milling, cement, shoes, tobacco and brewing, but the markets were too small. With tens of thousands of Africans in the surrounding villages earning very little in hard cash, the goods produced were not sold in sufficient quantities to make an industry pay. Capital to set up the industries had come from abroad, but wealthy investors did not like the small returns on their money, and they also became frightened when political troubles flared up in places like the Congo, Algeria and Nigeria. Another difficulty was that some of the industries employed too few people. An oil refinery in western Nigeria has a great deal of equipment, but employs only a thousand people for each million pounds invested, as most of the workings are automated; yet every year 100,000 children leave western Nigerian schools seeking employment.

People and how to look after them: this is the greatest problem. Clearly if they are wanted in industry, they must come to

African house in Rhodesia provided under a government scheme. It is a solid, three-room building with some garden space, but great estates of them are often built at considerable distances from work

the towns. There must be the transport to move them, homes to house them, schools to train them. Here is the tragedy of modern Africa. In many places they are neither housed, nor trained, nor given welfare services, and in some places not even employed. Why do they come?

Like Europeans and Americans an African has learned to ask more from life. He sees the town as a means of escape from the traditional life of the tribe and village, and as an outlet for his energy. In particular, he is drawn by the rumour of work and money, and he arrives with rising expectations. He will, he hopes, now be able to pay his taxes, educate his children, buy shirts, trousers, bicycles and beer for himself, and pots and pans and gay dresses for his wife. He needs to send sheets of tin back home to his family, for a tin roof on a mud hut has become a village status symbol. Also, one writer has judged life in a city to be 'a modern form of initiation rite; a youth cannot expect to win a girl's favour unless he can show the brand of the town'.

He is soon disillusioned. He finds lodging at a 'hotel' where he shares a room with five others for about 2s. 6d. a week. He has to get his own food and bedding. Jobs are hard to find for he hasn't the skill and there is much competition. He might get some manual work for 12s. a week. Only a very lucky and thrifty man manages, after a long time, to afford a tiny plot of land on which to build a hut, so that he can send for his wife and children. But once he does this, he loses the support which his village community and family kinship gave him.

A 1957 survey in the East African city of Kampala revealed elegant streets flanked with trees, but also showed part of the urban surroundings these people lived in:

'Roads, drainage and water supply are lacking; such roads as do exist are deeply-ravined stretches of ground with standing pools of water across which a few lorries and cars bump crazily. Water could only be obtained from three or four natural springs. Some households fetch it themselves, but most buy it at 10 cents a large tin from a water seller.'

African towns such as this have three sorts of labourers: a few landless families, living permanently in rented rooms; a 'commuter' group—men and women who come into town from a nearby village to work for a few hours as clerks or domestic servants before returning home; and men who migrate for a period of years to a town from distant, overcrowded villages to earn some cash before going back home. Many of this last group are what Europeans call 'target workers'. They work until they have saved enough to buy something like a bicycle, and then they return home until they find they want something else. African city officials and the well-to-do dread the growing numbers of these migration workers. If jobs are scarce they roam around the 'shanty towns' encircling a city, becoming, says one writer, 'a huge, unemployed, unhygienic, starving, thieving mob'. The size of the problem in cities like Cairo and Lagos is already frightening, and Kinshasa (Leopoldville), which used to be an interesting, bustling town with its shops, markets and cafés, has in the 1960s become 'drowned by numbers and a refugee city'.

All this is rather difficult to realize considering Africa is a relatively empty continent. A high density of population is found only in a few places such as the South African cities and ports, the Nile Valley, southern Nigeria, the shores of Lakes Victoria and Malawi, the slopes of mountains Kenya and Kilimanjaro and a few other coastal areas. The problem in these areas is simply expressed. Africans are hurrying into the modern world, and the traditional ways of life with their handicrafts, old transport and old-fashioned service are losing young men too rapidly. But modern industry and commerce uses so much machinery and skill that they cannot absorb all those who want jobs.

Ibadan

Ibadan, in Nigeria, has a million people, and is the largest 'African' city (as opposed to 'European-occupied') south of the Sahara. It used to be called 'the city of sixteen gates and seventy blacksmiths', and even today Ibadan is alive with the activities of craftsmen. Local people refer to it as a 'city village', because huge areas of it are peopled by traders and craftsmen living and working in a way closely resembling the African village. On the outskirts farming is still done with the hoe and axe; yet Ibadan has a highly modern commercial centre and big manufacturing industries. New offices, shops, factories and schools surround the old quarter of the city. For example, around the blacksmiths (there are today 240 of them), spinners, weavers, soapmakers and carpenters have been established canneries for local fruit, a large cigarette company, a foam-rubber factory and a printing corporation.

Mr Acquah is a typical resident of Ibadan. He left school in 1938 after only four years there because his family was too poor. He went into his carpenter-brother's business and worked hard; by 1952 he had married and saved £50 which enabled him to set up on his own as a furniture maker. In 1963 he employed two men and was training apprentices. Rent for his workplace only cost him 30s. a month, and with such low overheads Mr Acquah, in ten years in business, managed to invest £300 in additional equipment for his workshop, and save £150 in the bank. He is ambitious, and knows if he is to compete on equal terms with a nearby furniture works specializing in contemporary Scandinavian designs he must keep up-to-date in his equipment and business methods.

Ibadan has its problems, but Mr Acquah represents the future hopes of the city, and perhaps for other African urban areas. By his slowly acquired skill and enterprise he has provided his family with a reasonably prosperous way of life. He has risen above the low standard of living out in the Nigerian villages, where an income of only £150 a year for a family of five is common. Yet he is not one of the westernized élite whose standards the ordinary Africans feel are out of their reach.

18 Trade–Who Benefits?

The Poor Nations of Africa

'Each developing country in Africa is like a man who wants to build a fleet of ships. First, he makes a rowing boat, and pulls and sweats carrying people across a river until he has enough profit to build a coaster. Then he takes his coastal steamer up and down the shores, until he can afford one ocean-going ship . . . then two, and soon a fleet. But if that rowing boat goes straight to the ocean, it sinks.'

In 1967 Julius Nyerere, President of Tanzania, made those remarks to a United Nations meeting. He argued forcibly that the world is divided into two, the rich and the poor. Poor nations cannot go out on to today's highly competitive commercial 'oceans' until, he said, 'the sea is made calmer'. To Nyerere's way of thinking, most of Africa is poor and underdeveloped. What does this mean, and why should this be so?

Mass poverty is nearly universal in Africa. Poverty can be described in many ways. Economists try to measure it by working out how much cash income a household earns in a year and dividing it by the number in the family (this is called 'income per head', and the United Kingdom national average in the 1960s would be around £500). Many people think the 'poverty line' is £70 per head, yet in many African countries the figure is well below this. If people have so little cash then their government cannot tax them efficiently. For instance, Ghana can only collect £15 for every person in the country. And the government of Sierra Leone has less money to spend than a single large British or American university. Africans have for centuries been used to paying tribute to their rulers, but this was usually in the form of goods and animals. This is of little use to a modern government which wants money for social services, such as schools and hospitals, and industrial development.

There is another, very real, way of describing poverty. Africa is short of adequate housing, clothing and food. Yet, says one expert, 'There is no reason to despair. Poverty is there, but

Starvation in Dahomey: two children discovered too weak to finish their journey to a UNO food distribution centre

scarcely anything to touch the filth and degradation of nine-teenth-century English towns. Shelter, warmth and clothing are not costly in the tropics.' Shortage of the right kind of food is more critical. Undernourishment and malnutrition are easily recognized. People have loose skin, which falls in folds on the upper arms, their ribs are clearly visible and their knees are knobbly, and the head looks too large in proportion to the rest of the body. The eyes are dead-looking. Kwashiorkor, a disease which results from too little protein in the diet, is wide-spread in rural Africa.

Africa is one of the largest land masses in the world. It has some great riches, producing 50 per cent of the world's gold, 98 per cent of diamonds, 60 per cent of cocoa and 65 per cent of the palm oil annually in the 1960s. Despite this, Africa has only one-twentieth of the world's trade, and is right at the bottom of the league table of commercial areas.

We have already seen some of the reasons for this poverty. First, the production of food and goods has in many areas remained at or only slightly above subsistence level. Secondly, the Europeans who controlled Africa in the colonial period, were only interested in easily marketed cash crops or minerals. There was little encouragement given to the African to set up his own manufactures. This was partly a question of money, for, as one writer says, 'European governments ran their colonies on shoe-string budgets'. It was also partly deliberate. The colonies were useful markets for European machine-produced consumer goods, such as clothes and household equipment.

Thirdly, until independence most of Africa's overseas trade in products like gold, coffee, copper and cocoa, was tightly controlled from Europe. The international marketing of cocoa, for instance, was done in London not Accra in the Gold Coast.

'Creditworthiness'

A traveller in Nigeria recently observed: ' In one market I know well there is a row of some eight men, all reasonably fit, whose work appears to be to sell about 100 tomatoes each in the course of a day. How much better if one were selling all 800 tomatoes (not an excessive task for a barrow-boy in an East End market in London), three growing more tomatoes and perhaps some corn as well, one was transporting the produce to market and the other three building roads or teaching.' This story illustrates a central difficulty of African trade: how to get people to transfer from the traditional market stall to the complexities of modern commerce. Some ambitious African traders are doing it with the help of credit from the big African-based European firms, either in direct cash loans or by allowing an African to take goods for sale if he is reliable.

But it is hard for many Africans to become 'credit-worthy'. Some European businessmen are suspicious of the African. A Rhodesian bank report declares, 'he is childishly simple, irresponsible and unreliable'. Another white man complained, 'Africans keep changing their names, and you can't identify them because they all look alike'. Apart from such prejudice, there is the more important problem of family attitudes. A small West African cocoa dealer is part trader, part farmer, and any loan or profit he makes in trading is liable either to be spent on the farm, or on the family in the form of a big car or an expensive house to impress the relatives.

So, before a trader can get credit, he has to work very hard on narrow profit margins. Some West African traders are offered only the low 1s. in the £ discount by foreign importers.

131

Bartering in an African market in Cameroon

As one writer says, 'Everything hangs on a quick turnover, a knowledge of market prices a hundred miles around and the selling in small quantities down to a single cigarette.'

Aid

Today, African countries need money from abroad, and both the western world and Communist countries have contributed. They see that making Africa prosperous in trade, agriculture and industry would be as useful to them as to Africa. But in the late 1960s intelligent African statesmen have appreciated that some aid has had in the past more prestige value than worth to the ordinary people. A great power station may be a sound investment for the *future*, but for the same money 100,000 bullock carts would be of more immediate help to Africans.

What Africans want is money and advice which will help them to help themselves. Priority must be given to agriculture, which needs to be more efficient. Kenya's example could be copied. She is adding horticulture of pineapples, beans and peas to coffee as an important source of export revenue; in 1968 flowers found their way from Kenyan farms to Covent Garden in London. Also big regional markets are being organized. The East African Common Market has been created for thirty million people, 'to make', says its organizer, 'industry possible'. These two developments are closely related, for Africans have realized the hard way that it is no good manufacturing goods if few people locally have enough cash to buy them.

Pre-colonial Africa had a flourishing local and overseas trade. After partition, Europeans tended to channel the benefits of trade away from Africa. Today, African governments have to solve the difficult problem of balancing the work on the farms, in the factory and in the shops and markets to benefit their own citizens directly.

19 On Women, Children and Education

A Woman's Place . . .

Before the twentieth century an African woman in many parts of Africa was completely dependent upon her husband. This was her status, for a woman's place was in the home, bringing up the children. This dependence was the result of many things. Dowries had to be paid; and a woman might be only one of several wives in African societies which were polygamous. Marriages, too, were always 'arranged' between families, so a woman rarely had a free choice of husband. Then there was the question of safety. Because, in many areas of the forest zones of Africa, men regarded only hunting and fishing as proper work, they left the care of the food crops to the women. Yet until the turn of the century the woman could not go to work in the fields or to a market without an armed escort because of the dangers from slave-raiding and the many local tribal wars. She could not, in any case, trade for herself or her family as there was rarely any acceptable small currency.

With the European colonial governments came their kind of law and order. Markets were opened up, and women were encouraged to grow and sell more. Cassava, for instance, was thought of as 'merely a woman's crop', beneath the dignity of a male. So in several African societies women took up their own jobs. As well as farming there was pot-making and market-trading. 'Nowadays,' said an old Nigerian woman, 'women can go to the fields and get cassava to sell. Then she can say, "What is man? I have my own money."' Such African women were no longer dependent on their menfolk for food. Over the years this produced a revolution in African standards of living: it slowly ended the hitherto constant threat of famine, and introduced small amounts of cash into the household, which could be saved for clothing, furniture and schooling.

Amongst some peoples, however, the 'emancipation' of women hardly started. Rebecca Njau, a Kikuyu woman from Kenya, expresses this in her poem:

Toil and sweat
What else is there?
Old women, dark and bent, trudge along
With their hoes to the weedy maize plots;
Young wives like donkey,
Go about their timeless duties.
Their scraggy figures like bows
Set in a row . . .

There are so many variations in status that generalizations are, of course, impossible. Travellers through West Africa only can see women working in the tribal fields with primitive tools, and contrast them with the elegant young women in the streets of Lagos; or the veiled Muslim wives of Kano with the 'market mammies' of Accra. So, by way of illustration, the rest of this chapter looks at only two countries, Nigeria and Kenya.

Marriage

Marriage is rarely a personal matter; in an African village it is still more of a 'contract' between two families. Bride price is a key feature of this contract (it is what a man pays to his wife's parents on marriage). It varies enormously. With some Kenya peoples it could be £50, paid in a mixture of cattle and cash; one tribe makes a clear distinction—fourteen head of cattle and £40 for an uneducated girl, but the cash figure is £75 for a girl with several years' schooling. In Nigeria in the mid-1920s Ibo bridewealth was about £10–£20; thirty years later in Ibo towns the sums had increased to £100 for a girl with no schooling and £300 for a nurse, teacher or midwife; yet in the rural areas it was still around £10 or even less!

Young, educated African women are annoyed at the system of bride price. 'It is too much like selling a woman,' they say. But one teacher, when questioned closely, said, after much hesitation, that she would still ask a marriage price for *her* daughter, because of 'the trouble she had taken in rearing her'.

An African village marriage has no parallel in western countries. An Englishwoman, Sylvia Ross, became interested in the subject and tried to find out if there was an actual ceremony. After lengthy investigations amongst the Ibo in Nigeria, she came to the conclusion the marriage was a process not an act. There seemed to be no particular point at which a girl became

6

a wife. A girl was 'affianced' when she was still a baby, and payment of the bride price was begun immediately by the 'husband's' family; yet a husband could still be paying it a year after his own first child had been born! The nearest thing to a special ceremony seemed to be just before a bride went to live in her husband's family compound. Her skin was 'cut' slightly in three rows from just below the throat to the pit of the stomach, and then two more rows half way round the waist. Whilst this was being done about twenty women stood around singing loudly. Explanations varied. Two answers Sylvia Ross received were that the 'cuts were for pretty' and that 'the blisters could be used as money in the next world'.

In the towns many Ibo women lost all contact with village life. In Port Harcourt the compound system had disappeared in favour of individual houses of a more or less European type. A woman who was a small trader describes her day:

'I get up as soon as I hear the 6 o'clock siren, and go to the factory to buy cloth, soap or perhaps oil and salt. I carry these goods to market and arrange them on my stall. I then quickly run home (leaving the stall in the charge of some boy or girl I am training) to prepare my husband's breakfast. When this is done I hurry back to market, and here I remain until 11.30 buying and selling. Then I go home to cook dinner. When this is over I run back to the market, and stay until 5.30 when I pack up for the day.'

This woman is probably happy with her lot. Not all are. In coming to the large towns African women have deprived themselves of the many advantages of village life. One writer has said, 'In almost all African societies the woman has a "kingdom" of her own' with certain duties, but also respect; yet when they go to the town they find they have lost the security of communal life. In Port Harcourt Sylvia Ross wrote, 'no one ever takes root. Men come with their wives to make money, not to settle. The house of their ambitions will be built later, in their own village within full view of envious relations.'

This sketch of African women in the second quarter of the twentieth century shows that modern times have brought some compensation; but there has been much family tension as well. Nowhere is this clearer than in the changes in education resulting from European influence.

Housebuilding in the traditional African manner

Education—for What?

There are three kinds of education in Africa. There is the old, tribal education; there are the remains of the colonial schooling, which varied according to how the European power saw African requirements; and there is the 1960s' attempt to find an education suitable to the needs of modern Africa.

The old education grew naturally out of the village and tribal ways of life. A child had to learn how to deal with the dangers of his surroundings and how to treat his fellows. He knew about weather lore and the skills of a spear, axe and hoe from old men. His mother taught him correct speech, behaviour and respect

137

for his elders. Throughout his childhood it was impressed on him that he could not live alone—he must 'conform', and accept the ways of the tribe. He lived in a world of kinship: his kin gave him security and, as we have seen, a sort of social insurance in sickness and old age. Law and ownership of land, too, were based on kinship. So the child learned the rites which kinship would demand through his life from birth to maturity, marriage and death.

Much of this education was informal. The home was the child's school, where he learned tribal legends and proverbs. (The reader might work out the meaning of these two Baluyia proverbs from Kenya: 'A person running alone thinks he is the fastest runner' and 'A small bird cannot advise a bigger one'.) This social education had a great emphasis on correct conduct and confidence. A traveller in East Africa in 1930 wrote, 'I have seen three children between four years and six quite competently preparing a meal with no supervision.' But severe tests of endurance were a more formal part of this education. Chagga boys in East Africa in the old days had to sleep in holes in the ground at night for nine months, often in the cold mountain air, and they were deliberately stung by nettles. A boy was required to go on a lonely expedition into the forest to kill a leopard with a bow and arrow. Bena girls, aged nine to thirteen, were ducked repeatedly in streams, or terrified by women pretending to fall dead at their feet and by the appearance of monsters.

This tribal education had the advantage of preparing a child for life in the community; it could not allow him to be ambitious and independent, or teach him to meet the needs of the modern world. So in the colonial years missions and 'European' schools taught the kind of things children in Europe were taught. This produced a small westernized élite in some colonies, but it was severely criticized for having little to do with African needs. Reading books had robins and snow scenes in them; history books had accounts of the Wars of the Roses; arithmetic problems dealt with taps, wallpaper rolls and trains. Few of these things had anything to do with many African children's environment.

In the 1960s African needs are being rethought. Questions are being asked such as, how many universities should a country have, whilst half of an age group gets no schooling at all? A few highly trained electrical engineers are needed for the power stations, but Africa wants men skilled in the fairly simple techniques of wooden bridge construction, laying laterite roads and building single-storey houses. Civil servants, especially, need a good secondary education if they are to deal with matters ranging from money for a new agricultural scheme to collecting information for government approval of a harbour extension. For this, says one writer, 'a developing continent must clearly learn to be practical'. Many of the young men of African towns, who now use much of their energies selling vegetables to passing motorists, need to be attracted to the Young Farmers' Clubs or to evening classes in craft and commercial subjects.

The problems are very great, especially for the new but poor African nations. A 1963 Report on East Africa described the difficulties of a young secondary school boy in trying to obtain a sound education. He had to leave his village and seek lodgings as near to the school as possible with friends—here he did household work for his keep. He rose at 5 o'clock, hauled

The Library of Makerere University College, Kampala, Uganda

water for the family, made the fire and dug his 'master's' patch of garden. Then he had some tea and food before walking two, perhaps even ten, miles to school. He returned to his lodgings at noon to haul more water (usually a mile or so distant) and do some more digging. After tea he began his private study, which he continued by paraffin lamp or candle light when it was dark.

In Africa parents have become convinced that education is the key to a good job and to family prestige. But it has its drawbacks. Secondary and college education usually means that children have to leave the rural areas for the towns, and, later, as men they are not returning to work on the farms and produce the food. The opportunities and leisure attractions of the towns are too tempting.

20 Apartheid

1948: a New Political Slogan

For the general election of 1948 the Nationalist Party in the Union of South Africa needed a powerful watchword in their bid to win control of the government. This party was supported by the descendants of the Dutch Boers, now calling themselves Afrikaners. Many of them wanted to be rid of the old British connection (the Union had been an independent member of the British Commonwealth of Nations since 1910), but more important they were generally agreed that the supremacy of the white man in the Union must be made permanent. Ever since the 1920s the rallying cry 'Black Peril' had been an important vote-catcher, but the Nationalist Party had never quite managed to obtain complete power.

In 1948 Paul Sauer, an important Nationalist, suggested a slogan which he hoped would give his party victory: apartheid. The word itself was only five years old, having been coined by the South African newspaper, *Die Burger*; literally it means 'apartness', the idea that the different races of the union should be separated, as far as possible. Sauer's election hopes were fulfilled. But many of the voters who gave the Nationalist Party their 1948 success knew they were voting for white domination when they supported separation.

Leading Nationalists had already worked out some of the details of apartheid, and the new government led by Dr Malan introduced a programme of laws. There were difficulties. It was easy, for example, to make separate entrances for whites and non-whites compulsory in railway stations and public buildings, but the idea of complete territorial separation was awkward. Malan knew the expanding industrial areas of South Africa needed a large supply of labour, which the black peoples in the towns easily provided. They had drifted gradually in from the countryside over the past forty years in search of employment, as the traditional tribal areas were becoming over-populated.

A Brief Who's Who

In 1960 the Union of South Africa had 17 million people, not a large population for an area twice as big as France. The figure is much the same today. The whites are descended either from the Dutch, British or other European immigrants, and amount to 20 per cent of the population ($3\frac{1}{4}$ million). The Afrikaner group, speaking Afrikaans, a form of Dutch, control the government, its civil service and its foreign policy, and is made up of the farmers and the skilled workers in the towns. The English-speaking third of the white population dominates the banks, the mining and industrial businesses and the largest cities of the country.

Black Africans number $11\frac{1}{2}$ million people, who speak related languages called Bantu. They are widely scattered: a third in the old tribal homelands, which lie in a gigantic horseshoe in the eastern part of the country; another third live on the land of the white farmers they work for; the rest work in the industrial towns like Johannesburg, Durban and Cape Town. The biggest Bantu group is the Xhosa (pronounced 'Kawsa'), who with the Zulu, Sotho and Tswana are the most advanced of the South African tribal peoples.

Also there are the Cape Coloureds, the descendants of mixed racial marriages between the early white settlers and Hottentot, Malay or Negro women. The last two came with batches of slaves brought from the East Indies and West Africa, and such marriages were encouraged in the early, seventeenth-century days of the settlement—well before the Boers and Bantus clashed in the 1770s along the line of the Fish River in today's Cape Province. The Coloureds number $1\frac{1}{2}$ million.

Finally there are 500,000 Asians, mostly of Indian descent, who are concentrated in Natal. They came originally to work in the sugar industry, and today they form a community which works hard to preserve its own traditions and way of life.

Bantustans

Malan's successor as prime minister was J. F. Strijdom. He said, 'I am being as blunt as I can. Either the white man dominates or the black man takes over.' In Strijdom's government was a man who for years had been working out a blue-print for apartheid: Dr Hendrik Verwoerd. Physically a big man, he had an aggressive personality and a formidable intelligence. He rose rapidly to a leading position in the Afrikaner government. As Minister for Native Affairs in the 1950s he began the process of 'setting the races apart', and he continued it when in 1958 he became prime minister. His policy was so different from the Union of South Africa's partners in Britain's multi-racial Commonwealth that in 1961 South Africa broke this final link with Britain and set up a Republic. Meanwhile Verwoerd put his scheme for separate Bantu states, or Bantu-stans, into practice in June 1959.

The map shows how these Bantu homelands were to be consolidated into nine tribal areas. In 1963 one of them, the Transkei where the Xhosa live, was sufficiently well organized to become South Africa's first Bantustan. Local self-government was granted to the Xhosa: voting at twenty-one years for their own parliament; their own budget, courts, education and welfare services; to govern the Transkei they had their own prime minister, assembly of tribal chiefs and civil service. The white South African government kept control only of such things as defence, banking and communications. This was the

Bantustans. The giant horseshoe area in which the Afrikaner governments plan to establish Bantu homelands

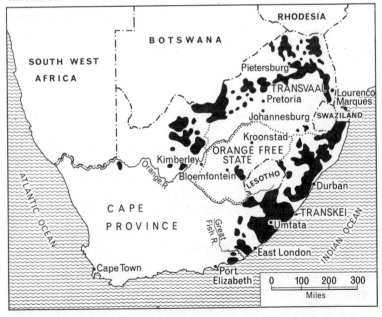

theory. In practice Afrikaners have kept strict control over most things in the Transkei.

But the chiefs of the neighbouring Zulu peoples have refused to cooperate in the Bantustan idea. In company with many other black Africans they are deeply suspicious of the Afrikaner government. In adding up the areas of the nine proposed Bantustans in the Republic, they find the total is only 13 per cent of the country, yet the non-whites are 80 per cent of the population; the Afrikaner inclusion of the ex-British territories of Lesotho (Basutoland), Botswana (Bechuanaland) and Swaziland to bring the area of the Bantustans to 42 per cent is regarded as a fraud. Doubts about Afrikaner sincerity have risen ever since the 1955 Report by a special committee to the South African government suggesting that £104 million should be spent on the Bantu Reserves for soil reclamation and to establish industries and a hundred new towns; the actual figure voted by the Afrikaner parliament was only £3 million. The most repulsive feature of the Bantustan scheme to the black Africans was the clause giving the South African government in Pretoria the power 'to choose, depose and veto'. A liberal South African newspaper, *The Golden City Post* protested at this. The Bantustans, it said, 'will be run by chiefs virtually appointed by Pretoria instead of freely-elected leaders'.

What of the Africans living outside the Bantustans? Many felt that a confidence trick had been played on them. There is the case of a Xhosa family living on the outskirts of Johannesburg: The husband was born in the city, grew up there and now works in one of its industries. But because *his* father came from the Transkei he is regarded as 'belonging' to it, and so he has the right to vote for the Transkei parliament, although he has never been there. In Johannesburg he has no such civil rights because he is 'one of the unattached mass of Bantu individuals', in fact a foreigner. He can, of course, take his family back to the Transkei, but in practice this would be impossible to do as well as maintain his standard of living, in view of the overcrowding and land shortage in the Bantustan.

Why? Afrikaners defend Apartheid

The following defence is based on the writings and speeches of some leading Afrikaners of the Nationalist Party of the Republic of South Africa:

'We care for our country. The evidence of the race riots and discrimination throughout the world in the 1950s and 1960s leads us to the conclusion that the different races cannot live closely together in harmony. People who hurl criticism at us think of the South African problem in terms of individuals, when they should think of *nations*. Do they really expect Zulu, Xhosa, Afrikaner and Englishman to live as one nation more readily than Frenchmen, Germans, Poles, Italians and Dutch?

'So what about the Bantu? He is human too isn't he? He has a right to his place in the sun, hasn't he? Our sensible answer to the problem of Bantu demands and Afrikaner nationalism is not to let the two meet. This is apartheid, though today we prefer to call it "separate development".

'So, three centuries later, we are setting up Bantustans, where the native can develop his own civilization. Perhaps there are a number of unpopular controls which we, as guardians, are exercising, but these are only in order to guide the natives.'

21 Sharpeville and After

The Black Reality

In 1960 Chief Albert Luthuli of Natal was awarded the Nobel International Prize for Peace. His speech at Oslo University during the Award ceremony condemned the Afrikaners' 'honeyed words' and their indifference to 'the sufferings of individual persons who lose their land, their homes, their jobs, in pursuit of what is surely the most terrible dream in the world'.

To black South Africans like Luthuli the Bantustans are a sham, and the government's policy is more accurately called 'white domination'. For in 1959 Verwoerd had said, 'We must safeguard White Man's control over our country.' In the fifteen years after their 1948 victory the Nationalists passed scores of laws which closely controlled what a non-white could do. They ranged from petty local regulations to national laws. In Johannesburg bye-laws are enforced for black domestic servants living in white homes: their own rooms must be concealed from the road in the back garden, and at least fifteen feet from the house; the windows of these rooms must be above eyelevel and small in size.

At work the whites dominate the skilled occupations and the non-whites the labouring tasks. In 1962 earnings for different groups were published. In mining the average white wage per year was £1,217, for coloureds £205, for Bantus £174; on the state railways wages were, £934 for whites, £163 for Bantus. Figures like these can be misleading. The educated whites brought to the industrial development of the nation money in the form of capital, skills and drive, whilst more than half the black labour force moved into the towns unable to read or write. Many 'poor white' Afrikaners who moved to the towns in the 1920s were also illiterate. But the black African feels that for him the real tragedy is a sense of *permanent* inferiority. For him there are few large-scale apprentice and training schemes. A leading African, Mphahlele, voiced his frustration: 'The White Man has de-tribalized me. He had better go the whole hog.'

146

A street in a poor quarter of Johannesburg

The practical symbols of a black man's inferiority are two discriminative documents. One he is denied for ever; the other considerably reduces his freedom of movement. The first is a green identity card, 4 inches by 3 inches, covered in cellophane, with a photograph, a nine-figure number and the vital letter 'W' on it. Families who have these are classified for all time as white, with all the privileges in housing, jobs and leisure facilities and the higher living standards in society that go with being white. For the rest there is a colour-bar to many of these privileges, and the second symbol, the pass laws. For many years non-whites had had to carry various 'passes', pieces of paper controlling their travelling, residence and employment. In 1952 a law consolidated all these into one Reference Book (it looks like a passport) which a non-white must carry at all times. He might find himself harassed and dragooned by police. 'Waar's jou pass, jong?' ('Where is your pass, boy?') is the question many adult Africans have to answer, and every year in South Africa a third of a million of them are fined or imprisoned for offences like entering a town to find work without permission, or failing to get a pass to be out after 10 p.m.

147

Passes being burned in a demonstration against the apartheid laws

Tragedy at Sharpeville 1960

African leaders were determined to force a showdown on the 'pass' system. So a non-violent demonstration was called for at Sharpeville, a small town near Vereeniging in south Transvaal. The idea was that Africans should hand in their passes at the local police station, so that by mass protest the system would break down.

In the early hours of 21 March 1960 men went through the streets of the town knocking on doors, seeking support. But as the number of demonstrators grew, it was clear that many did not have much idea of what they had to do. By 8 o'clock a small crowd had gathered at the fence around the police head-quarters. Some had come to protest about passes, others thought this was an opportunity to shout about police intimidation; but many said later that they were just idly curious. The crowd grew bigger, but there is no record of any policeman asking the people *why* it was there, or asking them to go away, yet at 10 o'clock several jet fighters flew over and then dived low towards the crowd in an effort to disperse them! The official police report afterwards claimed there were 20,000 Africans present, but photographs by some European pressmen suggest that 5,000 was a more correct figure.

At 1.15 p.m. Lt. Col. Pienaar, a senior police officer arrived. He said subsequently that he believed the crowd to be 'riotous and aggressive' and that a baton charge would not have scattered it. Yet, other photographs were produced to show the crowd to be 'in an idle, holiday mood, noisy, but with no weapons'.

At 1.30 Pienaar ordered the police to line up with weapons about five yards from the police station fence. The order 'Load five rounds' was given—Pienaar thought this would frighten the crowd. The next minutes were confused. Although no official command was issued, the word, 'Fire' was clearly heard, and the police reacted immediately. They fired wildly for about forty seconds: the ammunition count after the event revealed that 705 rounds had been used, so that some policemen must have reloaded their weapons. Also medical evidence showed that over half the victims were shot in the back as they were fleeing from the scene. Sixty-seven Africans were killed and 186 injured.

Why? An official enquiry into the Sharpeville shooting concluded that police action was 'deliberate and unnecessary', that it was due to prejudice, hatred, fear and contempt. It disclosed that Africans were thought of as a 'mob', never as persons. Pienaar, a policeman with thirty years' experience, said in his evidence: 'Native mentality does not allow them to gather for peaceful demonstrations. For them to gather means violence.'

In the light of such remarks some black Africans felt the peaceful protests of men like Luthuli were a waste of time.

Nelson Mandela: 'The Black Pimpernel'

After Sharpeville life could never be quite the same for the racial groups in South Africa. A state of emergency was declared by the government, thousands arrested and African political parties banned. But this only drove African leaders directly to violent action. Terrorist organizations like 'The Spear of the Nation' and 'Poqo' were formed. The Afrikaner government reacted to some sporadic sabotage by passing the

The Sharpeville shootings: *above*: Africans flee from police (one is standing on a

acen tank, right centre background); *below:* a few minutes later.

Ninety-Day Law, by which anyone could be arrested merely on *suspicion* of having terrorist information, kept in solitary confinement for ninety days, released and immediately re-arrested. Three thousand were detained under this law. Evidence was slowly collected about the key figures in the African secret organizations, and it led to the arrest in Rivonia, a suburb of Johannesburg, of eighteen white and black Africans. The date was July 1963.

The Rivonia Trial, which followed, attracted worldwide attention because of the defence of Nelson Mandela. A lawyer by training, Mandela was physically a big man with a commanding personality. He was known as 'The Giant' to his friends, but called 'The Black Pimpernel' by Africans from the way in which he had managed to keep out of police hands for so many years.

At the trial the men arrested were accused of planning violent revolution. They admitted this, but Mandela had chosen a form of defence allowed in the South African courts of law whereby the accused could speak uninterrupted from the dock. Mandela did so—for five hours. He stated the real issue: were people who were prevented from claiming their rights as human beings justified in using force?

'I planned sabotage as a result of a calm assessment of the political situation that has arisen after many years of tyranny, exploitation and oppression of my people by the whites. . . . Fifty years of non-violence had brought the African people more repressive laws and even fewer rights. . . . We fight against poverty and the loss of human dignity. Africans want to be paid a living wage. Africans want to perform work which they are capable of doing. . . . African women want to be with their menfolk, and not left permanently widowed in the reserves. . . . I have cherished the idea of a democratic and free society in which all people live together in harmony and with equal opportunities.'

His last words were: 'It is an ideal for which I am prepared to die.' They were spoken quietly, with great feeling, to a silent courtroom. It was a powerfully argued personal defence, but the verdict was guilty. Nelson Mandela and seven others were sentenced to life imprisonment on Robban Island, a close detention prison near Cape Town.

South Africa Approaching 1970

The Republic of South Africa is the strongest state on the continent. Its military power could resist a combined attack by all the other African states put together. Its prosperity is also greater than anywhere else in Africa, and it is nearly self-sufficient. The Republic has been stock-piling the only natural commodity of importance that it lacks: oil. By 1970 it is estimated that it will have about seven years supply stored away.

It also presents a contrast to the rest of Africa in the 1960s. Whereas Black Africans north of the Zambezi have been gaining independence from white rule and recognition of their human rights, in the Republic these rights are denied to many people by the Afrikaner government. In the late 1960s there seems little chance of a change of policy. In any case, as two authorities on African history, Roland Oliver and J. D. Fage, remark: ' Race relations have deteriorated too far to be mended by anything short of a miracle.'

22 The Future '... in which all persons live together'

Uboma

Mandela's words, quoted in the title of this chapter, imply that the basic problem in Africa is the human one: how to get people to understand and accept the best that the modern world can offer them. To find out what was best for a particular area and how to persuade people to change, an investigation, which could well be repeated in many places in the future, was begun in Uboma in 1962. Uboma is a group of six villages in the rain forest belt of Eastern Nigeria. It lies half-way between Enugu, the provincial capital, and Port Harcourt. Throughout its 25 square miles 30,000 people live in what appears to be forest, but is in fact farmland. The Shell Oil Company of Nigeria backed the project financially, and it was organized by the University of Ibadan. The field work was carried out by a thirty-year-old Ibo agriculture expert, Walter Ézeilo. Experience in other parts of the world showed that it was useless merely to examine crops, soils, climate, tools and cultivation methods; such things as markets, land ownership, could the people read, did they buy on credit, how hard they worked for how much reward—all these needed looking at as well.

The Ibos of Uboma earn their living by farming. They grow their own food, eating mostly starchy root vegetables like cassava and yams, with variety introduced by maize, beans and groundnuts. They get a little protein from fish and meat, but the second has to be bought at a market as the tsetse fly prevents large-scale pastoral farming. Ezeilo worked out that each person had less than 2,400 calories a day, a figure too low for growing children and nursing mothers. Thus he found a great deal of hookworm and bleeding gums among people during the 'hungry season' between March and June, which is early in the rainy season. Also, there were powerful religious taboos against certain food. Pythons and vultures, which could have made useful foods, were forbidden, and pregnant women might not eat owl or monkey meat in case a child was born with a similar face!

Cassava was a family food crop, but some of it had to be sold to increase the household income. The other main cash crops were the oil palm, bananas and cocoa. Exact records were kept of these and a very low yield was revealed. For instance, Uboma

Harvesting the oil palm in Uboma, Nigeria

produced only 320 lb of groundnuts per acre compared with Japan's 1,960 lb. Each household had about 165 oil palms in its half dozen acres; the return per tree in a year was only 2*s*. Thus when all the household income from farming was added to the little trading which the women did, it came to £156. As the average number in the household was six, this meant that Uboma's yearly income per head was the extremely low figure of £26.

Costs in Uboma, of course, are low, but Ezeilo had to take the £156 into account when he considered who was to pay for 'improvements'. Houses were cheap. The traditional, rectangular, mud-walled and rafia/bamboo roofed hut was usually built by the family. A contractor might charge £10 for the walls, £10 for doors and windows, £5 for the roof and furnishings would add another £5. The few modern houses in Uboma cost about £500. The family also had to find money for the bride price, which averaged £50 although £200 was not uncommon for an educated girl. Church dues, school fees, clothes and bicycles were other items demanding cash. On the practical side a small piece of machinery, the oil press, was highly prized as a more efficient way of extracting the palm oil.

Ezeilo thought three things were necessary as immediate improvements: more profitable cash crops were needed, the amount and variety of food must be increased and more animal protein was vital for the diet. This was not simply a matter of machinery, for the people could not afford it, and the key feature of the scheme at Uboma was that the farmer must see that it was his own efforts that led to improvement. By 1965 the first stage of the plan was under way. Chemicals for fertilizers and pest control were brought in at low cost. A new type of cassava was tried out by eighty farmers: yields went up by 16 per cent, and then tomatoes and onions were introduced. But Ezeilo's greatest successes were with the fishpond and the co-operative.

A government loan of £60 was given to clear the forest and prepare a five-acre fishpond. This not only produced a necessary source of protein, but also introduced irrigated rice paddy to Uboma. Then, with the local schoolmaster's leadership, a multi-purpose cooperative was set up. Here the project found the community's own tradition useful. Uboma has long had an

The middleman. This man in Uboma hires out his bicycle for transporting oil palm produce to market

'Isusu' Club, a kind of credit organization in which each member of a group of twelve (usually about the same age) put 10s. every market day into a pool, and the £6 was given to one member in turn to buy something big. Ezeilo thus found the idea of a community 'Coop' was easily accepted.

In only two years the Uboma Project showed what can be done without expensive equipment and without major changes in the village way of life. Uboma is a challenge to Africans. But

Uboma was not an isolated community, where experiment could be undertaken free from all the other tensions of African life. In 1967 it was caught up in the tragic story of Biafra.

Fears of Race War

In the mid-1960s Nigeria was regarded as the 'anchor' of independent Africa. It had had five years of peace since the end of the British colonial rule, and with its able prime minister, Tafawa Balewa it seemed to have formed a successful federation of such widely different peoples as the Ibos, the Yorubas and the Hausas. But the government in Lagos was dominated by the northern Hausas, and in 1966 a group of Ibo officers seized control. Balewa was killed and more army revolts took place after a massacre of an Ibo minority in Northern Nigeria.

The main body of Ibos in the south-east were led by Colonel Ojukwu, and on 30 May 1967 he took this area out of the Federation. This secession created a new state, Biafra. Federal Nigeria refused to recognize Biafra, and a thirty-two month long civil war broke out. Black fought black in a savage struggle about a form of government and the rights of minorities. Civilized men have done this for hundreds of years; but in Africa the situation is complicated by fears of white versus black.

Most of Africa south of the River Zambezi is ruled by white men. This bloc (the Republic of South Africa, Rhodesia and the Portuguese colonies of Angola and Mozambique) is more prosperous, stronger militarily and has better developed resources than Black Africa. Tension has risen a great deal in the 1960s between black and white areas. Guerrilla warfare, even, has developed at several places along the Zambezi 'frontier', and in 1968 the OAU (Organization for African Unity) voted £$\frac{3}{4}$ million to support such action against white supremacy. From a headquarters in Zambia in December 1968 a guerrilla leader claimed that small armed bands of about thirty black Africans are infiltrating to the south. Few battles are fought in this shadowy conflict; the guerrillas, trained for fast-moving bush fighting, claim they are engaged in a prolonged contest, in which they hope their sporadic, small-scale actions will wear down Rhodesian, Portuguese and South African resources.

Opinion abroad varies on the future. Open race war is possible. On 13 March 1968 the British newspaper, *The*

A representation of the struggle for power in the Africa of the 1960s

Guardian wrote: 'Failure to resolve the Rhodesian question can only lead to an extended form of civil war covering all southern Africa.' However, Europeans tend to see Africa as a continent full of problems: of civil war, colour bars and poverty. But for the ordinary man-in-the-street in Africa everyday life goes on and is of more practical concern. Some Africans are optimistic. 'There will be no race war,' said Dr Hastings Banda. 'Pay no attention to it.' And in 1968 Malawi was the first independent black African state to cooperate openly with the Republic of South Africa.

With threats of racial violence on the one hand, and 'live and let live' pleas on the other he would be a rash man indeed who could predict the future of Africa.

A Note on Words

Many readers of this book are probably aware by now that there are certain words which are convenient and brief to use, although they are really 'labels' for something more complex. Also, that there are some words which have a second, rather nasty, pejorative, meaning in which the user is condemning.

For example, *African, European* and *Arab*. The first usually means a black person born in Africa, but there are many white Africans with many generations of African life behind them; but, then, is an Arab from Algeria an African? 'European' is another curious word in that it can mean any white person, including American tourists from New York and Afrikaner settlers in Kenya!

Black, White and *Coloured* present similar difficulties. The last one for instance can mean either anyone not white or, as in the Republic of South Africa, a person descended from a mixed racial marriage.

Native, kaffir and *bush* are often used as terms of contempt, and because of this some people deliberately avoid them. 'Bush' can simply mean 'the countryside, scrub or forest' or 'a dull, primitive, uncomfortable way of life'.

Similar contrasts in meaning are found with words like *old, traditional* and *modern*. The first two used to describe something which has stood the test of time and was worth respecting, but today can be used for that which is out-of-date or out-worn. By the same argument 'modern' can be new, jazzy and useful.

Finally, the reader might think about the terms *nation* and *tribe*. Which should be used for Pygmies, Norwegians, Ibos, Poles, Hausas, Somalis, Irish? And why?

Further Reading

The literature of modern Africa is enormous and increasing.
Here are a few books to read which are interesting, accurate and
give good descriptions or explanations. Most of them are fairly
cheap and are in paperback. After these try some of the
excellent publications in the Penguin African Series.

BOYD & VAN RENSBERG, *An Atlas of African Affairs* (Methuen
    1965)
RUTH FIRST, *117 Days* (Penguin)
BRIAN GARDNER, *Mafeking: A Victorian Legend* (Sphere 1967)
ROBIN HALLETT, *Peoples and Progress in West Africa* (Pergamon
    1966)
GUY HUNTER, *The Best of Both Worlds* (OUP 1967)
ELSPETH HUXLEY, *Four Guineas* (Chatto and Windus 1955)
C. P. KIRBY, *East Africa* (Benn 1968)
PETER MANSFIELD, *Nasser's Egypt* (Penguin 1965)
PRINCE MODUPE, *I was a Savage* (Museum 1958)
OLIVER AND FAGE, *A Short History of Africa* (Penguin 1966)
BARBARA TOY, *The Way of the Chariots* (Murray 1965)
ESTHER WARNER, *Trial by Sasswood* (Pan)

You will find the photographs in Basil Davidson's *Africa,
History of a Continent* (Weidenfeld & Nicolson 1966) well worth
looking at. The book is expensive, but most libraries will have
a copy.

The School of Oriental and African Studies, University of
London produces a reading list for schools on African History.

Index

Page reference to Maps: